MW01074363

CONFESSIONAL, CONVICTIONAL, CHEERFUL BAPTISTS

NATE AKIN

Confessional, Convictional, Cheerful Baptists

ISBN 978-1-955295-47-5

Requests for information or permissions should be addressed to:

100 Manly Street
Greenville, South Carolina 29601
CourierPublishing.com

PUBLISHED IN THE UNITED STATES OF AMERICA

ENDORSEMENTS

This little book is filled with joyful orthodoxy from beginning to end. What a great call for us to be clear on what we believe and to be happy about it. Speaking as an SBC lifer, Nate gives a compelling call for us to be genuinely convictional in our Baptist distinctives and thoroughly pleasant in how we discuss them. I loved every page of this book and will gladly recommend it to every SBC pastor and church member I know!

Clint Pressley
Pastor, Hickory Grove Baptist Church

First off, let me affirm that Baptists should be confessional, convictional, and cheerful. Nate Akin had the good sense to put them together in this book, and to present a vision of Baptist identity for the 21st century that truly demonstrates those three identity markers. It is no small achievement that Baptists of every generation will recognize the authenticity and helpfulness of Nate Akin's argument. When faithful, Baptists embody confessional truth, convictional unity, and a cheerful disposition. The great insight of this book is that no two of these will survive the absence of the third. So read it confessionally, convictionally, and cheerfully — and soon.

R. Albert Mohler Jr., President
The Southern Baptist Theological Seminary, Louisville, KY

Winston Churchill wrote, "Those that fail to learn from history are doomed to repeat it." To try and avoid the mistakes of the past, we must first learn history. For the Christian, studying history allows us to see how God is guiding all things to his appointed ends for his glory. Second, we must learn from history. From history, we can learn how earlier generations responded to their own challenges, which gives us insight into how we may respond to our own. In Confessional, Convictional, Cheerful Baptists, Nate Akin reminds us of our Baptist history in order to learn from it how to navigate the challenges facing us. In a time when we're tempted to blur the lines of what we believe in order to "win souls," we need to be reminded that what makes us Baptist is just that — what we believe. If we are to maintain the faith that has been delivered to us from previous generations of Baptists, we must remember what we believe, why we believe it, and how to maintain it.

Juan R. Sanchez
Senior Pastor, High Pointe Baptist Church, Austin, TX

DEDICATION

This book is dedicated to my mom (Charlotte) and dad (Danny) who have from childhood acquainted us "with the sacred writings." You have taught me what it means to love Baptist doctrine and people. Those people who love Christ, His Church, and His Commission.

CONTENTS

ACKNOWLEDGMENTS

This book would not have been written without the help, support, and encouragement of my bride Kelsey Akin, Evan Knies (Book Publisher at Courier Publishing), Kevin Simmons (Director of Operations at the Pillar Network), Phil Newton (Director of Pastoral Care and Mentoring at the Pillar Network), Eric Smith (Associate Professor of Church History at The Southern Baptist Theological Seminary), Jeff Robinson (President of Courier Publishing), Alex Duke (Editor at Courier Publishing), Lauren Spano (Editor at Courier Publishing), and Denise Huffman (Editor at Courier Publishing).

PREFACE

I am no Renaissance man — nor are the other men in my family. I can't fix things. I can't cook, draw, paint, or sing. I'm a pretty simple man and can speak intelligently about only a few things: sports and theology and occasionally TV sitcoms. And yet, those who know me best would say I get most passionate talking about Georgia football and what it means to be a Baptist. I'm a man of concentric circles. First, I'm a Christian who joins with all the redeemed. I affirm the Apostles Creed, Nicaea, and the tenets of the Reformation. Second, I'm a Baptist — in what follows I will seek to show why. Third, I'm a Southern Baptist and still believe passionately in the work we are doing together for the propagation of the gospel in all nations. Finally, I'm a Pillar Network Baptist.

Pillar is a Reformed-leaning Baptist network that is made of Southern Baptist Churches in the U.S. and Baptist churches around the world who are committed to gospel proclamation; the sufficiency of the Bible; live, expository preaching; qualified, male elder plurality; confessional Baptist polity; and kingdom-mindedness (commitment to cooperation among like-minded local churches for planting and revitalization rather than just growth). In what follows, it will be helpful to know who I am, where I'm coming from, and what I'm passionate about.

How did I find myself within those concentric circles? First, I was born into a family with a long Southern Baptist heritage. I heard the gospel weekly in Southern Baptist churches. I was baptized in the Audelia Road Baptist Church in Garland, TX. My dad has served Southern Baptist churches or institutions my entire life. I was born in it, and I was raised in it.

Then, as is often the case, I experienced a crisis of faith. After a time of sin, repentance, and reflection, I began to ask myself some probing questions about what I really believed. Among those questions was "Am I really a Baptist?" Thankfully, because of my upbringing, I knew I could only answer that question by investigating the Scriptures. So that's what I did — and, over time, I realized I was not only convinced by but also excited about Baptist doctrine. Though I am certainly a believer in sovereignty and providence, you might say I once was a Baptist by chance but now I am a Baptist by conviction. It's that conviction that prompted this book. The first occasion for much of this book was a sermon at the annual Pillar Network Unite Conference. I called the sermon, "Convictional, Confessional, Courageous, Compassionate, Cheerful, and Corinthian Baptists." That sermon was borne out of a burden not only to hold strongly to what we believe but to do so in a distinctly Christian way. I want us Baptists to really be Baptists! I want us to have strong convictions but to hold to them joyfully and not like jerks. And yet, when I say "us," I know I'm really preaching to myself. I recognize my own temptations and faults. I know the secrets of my heart and how I often want to respond to others with whom I disagree. Right before I preached the sermon that inspired this book, Dwayne

Milioni, one of the co-founders of the Pillar Network, described me as a man with a "single-minded devotion." Other friends say things like "You are the most committed Baptist I know" or "You can be quite convictional on these things." In my zeal for these things I hold dear, I'm tempted to be proud and dismissive of others who aren't as "enlightened" as I am. This is a danger for anyone with strong convictions about anything, Baptists included.

Which is why, when I think of being so decidedly Baptist, 1 Corinthians dominated my mind. Paul's letter is a good place to start because it contains our most cherished Baptist beliefs, but it also reminds us that we are now saved sinners. As a zealous believer and fallen sinner, I'm still so thankful that "such *were* some of you" (1 Cor 6:11). It's this recognition of undeserved grace that helps season our convictions with humility and cheerfulness.

That's the background for this book. I pray it serves the concentric circles I described. As I will unpack *why* later in the book, I pray it also helps many be more happily and decidedly Baptist for the sake of Christ, His Church, and His Commission.

FOREWORD

It is not often that a father gets the privilege of writing the foreword to a book authored by his son.

Gratefully, I am honored to have this opportunity.

Nate Akin loves our Lord's churches, especially those which have Baptist in their name.

He reads widely in the area of Baptist distinctives and ecclesiology and is continually challenging this tradition to think well concerning what the church is, what the church does, and how the church conducts itself.

Nate takes very seriously 1 Timothy 3:15, that followers of Christ "may know how one ought to behave in the household of God, which is the church of the living God, a pillar and buttress of the truth."

You see, when it comes to being a faithful witness at any time and in any place, it is crucial that the churches which faithfully follow Jesus believe the truth but also live the truth.

They must be convictional and faithful on the one hand. And they must be courageous, compassionate, and cheerful on the other.

They must hold tightly what they believe with a smile, not a frown.

As Colossians 4:6 admonishes us, "Let your speech *always* (emphasis mine) be gracious, seasoned with salt, so that you may know how you ought to answer each person."

The Message colorfully reads, "The goal is to bring out the best in others in a conversation, not put them down, not cut them out."

Those words, unfortunately, don't always sound like the Baptists.

They are, however, the Bible!

Striking the balance between firm convictions and heartfelt compassion is not always easy. Being full of grace and truth is a challenge.

However, it is always essential if we are to witness well to those outside the church and to serve well those inside the church. Nate Akin has written an excellent book pointing us in the right direction.

It is helpful and it is needed.

Daniel L. Akin
President, Southeastern Baptist Theological Seminary

INTRODUCTION

As we think on the topic of being decidedly Baptist, it seems appropriate to alliterate this book's title. Hopefully this title will also describe clearly who we are.

My father, Danny Akin, has said many times, "What you say is most important, but how you say it has never been more important." With this sentiment in mind, I'm concerned for the broadly Reformed stream of many confessional Baptists. Social media and other avenues have created what can only be described as a firestorm of people building platforms based on being angry about their convictions. A leading Southern Baptist recently said to me, "Sadly if a messenger gets up to speak and his church has the name 'Grace' in it, you can almost guarantee he won't be very gracious." Another said on Twitter, "If someone's bio has 1689 in it, although a wonderful confession, you can likely mark it down that he will be angry or haughty." He's referring to the Second London Confession of 1689 (2nd London). Many confessional Baptists don't fully subscribe to the *2nd London*, yet they do subscribe to the doctrines of grace it describes. For brothers and sisters with these convictions, these things ought not be so.

Much of what I write may be preaching to the choir. That's fine. I'm certainly preaching to myself as one who holds so staunchly the convictions in this book. Truthfully, the doctrines of grace should make us gracious. The doctrines of grace should make us happy. If we claim to be Reformed, we should also be warm. As Baptists — as those who hold clearly to a regenerate faith and practice a baptism that symbolizes our death to sin, union to Christ, and resurrection to an eternal life in Him — we should be of all people most happy. The goal of this book is to consider what it means to be convictionally, confessionally, and cheerfully Baptist — to consider what we hold dear, why we hold it dear, and how we can hold it well. In doing so, let's start in 1 Corinthians 16:13–14. I lead a church-planting organization, which means I see all kinds of church names. There was a time when it seemed like every church plant seemed to start with the letter *R*. We saw a lot of Redemptions, Restorations, Redeemers, and even some Remnants. Then every new church seemed to evoke mountain peaks. So you had your Summits, Pinnacles, or The Hill. Some even saw the need to combine the two. So you got *Redemption Hill*.

But you know what name I have yet to hear? Corinth Baptist Church! Now, Corinth Baptist churches *do* exist, and they even exist in cities not named Corinth. But it's not a popular name, and for good reason, because the church at Corinth was a mess.

And yet, in that mess perhaps we see something of our own mess. Perhaps we have a lot to learn from what might be called a troubled and yet triumphant church, which can be said of all churches on this side of glory. As we approach our subject at hand, consider who wrote these verses for us: a man formerly named Saul, a "persecutor of the Way," who is now named Paul. This transformed man writes these words under the inspiration of the Holy Spirit, "Be watchful, stand firm in the faith, act like men, be strong. Let all that you do be done in love" (1 Cor. 16:13–14).

Here we have a sinner, saved by undeserved grace, encouraging the saints in Corinth to essentially be confessional, convictional, courageous, and compassionate. Let's consider then what we hold dear and how we can hold it well.

CONFESSIONAL, CONVICTIONAL, CHEERFUL BAPTISTS

PART 1

WHAT WE HOLD
DEAR AND WHY

Chapter 1

CONVICTIONAL AND CONFESSIONAL BAPTISTS

(1 Corinthians 16:13a)

"Be watchful, stand firm in the faith…"

In 1 Corinthians 16:13a, Paul exhorts believers to be convictional or resolute in what they believe: "Be watchful and stand firm in the faith." In two verses, he gives five succinct commands. We'll focus on the first two: "be watchful" or "alert" or, maybe even more pointed, "vigilant."

The world constantly throws worldviews at us that compete with the Christian faith. Even worse, our own sinful hearts feel pulled away from the true object of our affection. So, Paul says, "Watch out!" He says the same thing to the Ephesian elders in Acts 20:31. After charging them to pay attention to themselves and to the flock of God, he says, "Therefore, **be alert,** because fierce wolves will come." Peter uses the same phrase in 1 Peter 5.

Why the repetition? Paul and Peter have learned this from our Lord who said the same thing to his disciples while on the road to

Calvary in Mark 13–14. This exhortation culminates in the Garden of Gethsemane when Jesus agonizes over what He is about to become for us. He simply says, "**Be watchful** that you may not enter into temptation. The Spirit indeed is willing but the flesh is weak."

Paul follows up "be watchful" with "stand firm in the faith." You could also translate it, "Be resolute." This is military language for "stand your ground." In our day of memes, think about the one with William Wallace (Mel Gibson) yelling, "Hold!" Here, Paul has in mind something like what our Lord's brother Jude writes, "Contend for the faith [that faith or that body of belief] that has been once and for all delivered to the saints." We must be convinced by the doctrines of the Scriptures. We must be committed not just for our own maturity, but for those saints under our care. Many commentators believe Paul has in mind here the specific doctrines that surround the gospel, what he has called in the previous chapter that "which is of first importance, that Christ died for our sins according to the Scriptures and was raised on the third day according to the Scriptures" (1 Cor. 15:3ff).

As Baptists, as we think about the Faith in which we must stand firm, our convictions and confessions remain a good place to start. We believe that Baptist doctrine most faithfully represents the New Testament. We also believe our distinctives help us to uphold and protect the gospel and what we believe about conversion. The gospel changes people, and changed people are the vehicle by which the gospel is spread to the world. These changed people do not undertake this mission as lone rangers but rather are saved into a people called the church. Baptists believe this reality becomes visible only through saved persons' connection to the local church. In other words, God's chosen means for gospel proclamation is the church which is the pillar and foundation of **the truth** (1 Tim. 3:15). The

Pastoral Epistles (1 and 2 Timothy, Titus) explain how sound doctrine brings spiritual health. We get our English word *hygiene* from it. The goal of starting and strengthening churches then is not to build a crowd. The goal is to saturate our people, our neighborhoods, and the nations with that which will make them healthy — namely, the gospel. This would mean that doctrines centered on the gospel, which we hold dear in our Baptist ecclesiological convictions, form the basis for our gospel ministry. In other words, we believe our Baptist ecclesiological convictions best form pillars of the truth.

At the Pillar Network, but also throughout the entire SBC, our doctrine drives our mission. We aren't doctrinally aligned just for the sake of stodgy confessionalism. We're aligned for evangelism. We believe our statements of faith have what the world needs most. That's why we're confessionally baptistic.

This now leads us to consider Baptist confessions, those statements of faith Baptists throughout history have used to clarify their most convictional beliefs.

Chapter 2

BAPTIST CONFESSIONS

The use of confessions comes right out of the Scriptures. Recall Paul's command to "stand firm in the faith." What is "the faith"? Confessions of faith answer this question. Other passages defend the practice, such as Jude 3, 2 Timothy 1:14, and 2 Thessalonians 2:15.[1]

Confessions are statements of belief that guide biblical interpretation for cooperation and identity. They serve as a way for us to say to a confused world, "This is what we believe."

It's not an exaggeration to say that in our world, confessions are necessary. In fact, faithful missions can't move forward without shared belief, and shared belief requires us to share that belief with the world. Confessions, then, provide boundaries for cooperation around the beliefs we will propagate to the world.

So what about Baptists and confessions? Well, Baptists have always been a confessional people.

---

1 B.H. Carroll helpfully points this out in his sermon on "Creeds and Confessions of Faith" from the book *Baptists and Their Doctrines* edited by Timothy and Denise George. *Baptist Confessions, Covenants, and Catechisms*. Broadman and Holman Academic, Nashville, TN, 79-105.

Since the 1600s, Baptists have written, in English alone, more than 25 well-known confessions. Confessions are in our Baptist blood. I don't just mean in America, but across countries and centuries. The preamble to the Baptist Faith and Message 2000 (BFM2000) states, "Throughout our history **we have been a confessional people**... . Each generation bears the responsibility of guarding the treasury of truth that has been entrusted to us... . Baptist churches, associations, and general bodies have adopted confessions of faith as a witness to the world, and as instruments of doctrinal accountability."

We might debate just how confessional the Southern Baptist Convention (SBC) is, but it cannot be debated that the Convention has had an adopted confession for the majority of its history. Pillar Network, which I serve, happily stands upon historic baptistic confessionalism to show that we stand in the line of our Baptist forebears. There has certainly been pushback on the use of confessions. Campbellites, as well as some Baptists, have been known for saying something akin to "no creed but the Bible."[2] Some Baptists who have pushed against confessions have done so because of an over-realized and poorly understood concept of soul competency; this replaced the priesthood of all believers with the priesthood of the individual believer. We'll address these Baptist distinctives later in the book. However, it's worth noting here that — almost without exception — religious experiments without a confession of faith have gone poorly and eventually led to theological liberalism.

The concept "no creed but the Bible" is inconsistent with the majority of our Baptist history and upended by Baptist doctrines themselves. Again, I will address this in detail later in the book. For

---

2 Dr. Albert Mohler addresses both groups and the dangers of this mindset in a Baptist21 Podcast: https://baptist21.podbean.com/e/episode-147-interview-with-dr-albert-mohler-on-confessions/

now, I'll simply refer us to Dr. Timothy George, who writes in his excellent work *Baptist Confessions, Covenants, and Catechisms*:

> Many of the framers of the confessions, covenants, and catechisms published in this volume would be hard pressed to recognize as their spiritual heirs certain present-day Baptists who advance an ideology of indifference to the great doctrines of the faith for which their forebearers suffered and sometimes died... . Many contemporary Baptists are surprised to learn that such venerable shapers of the Baptist tradition as Andrew Fuller, James P. Boyce, B.H. Carroll, and E.Y. Mullins used the word "creed" in a positive sense and often spoke in an affirming way "the Baptist creed." It is nonetheless true that Baptists have never advocated creedalism... . Baptists are not creedal in that they have never elevated any man-made doctrinal construct above Holy Scripture... . The Bible alone remains the **norma normans** for all teaching and instruction, "the supreme standard by which all human conduct, creeds, and religious opinions should be tried." ... Despite this aversion to creedalism, however, the idea that voluntary, conscientious adherence to an explicit doctrinal standard is somehow foreign to the Baptist tradition is a peculiar notion not borne out by careful examination of our heritage.[1]

He also quotes the 18th-century Baptist theologian Andrew Fuller:

> It has been very common among a certain class of writers, to exclaim against creeds or systems in religion as inconsistent with Christian liberty and the rights of conscience; but every well-informed and consistent believer must have a creed, a system which he supposes to contain the leading principles of divine revelation... . If the articles of faith be opposed to the authority of Scripture, or substituted in the place of

---

1 George, *Baptist Confessions, Covenants, and Catechisms*, 2-3.

such authority, they become objectionable and injurious; but if they simply express the united judgment of those who voluntarily subscribe them, they are incapable of any such imputation.[2]

Further, Dr. Albert Mohler speaks about the need for the Abstract of Principles (Abstract) which is The Southern Baptist Theological Seminary's (SBTS) founding Confession. This confession arose to combat the dangerous Campbellite theology previously mentioned, which argued for "no creed but the Bible."[3] Mohler addresses why the need for a Confession was important to J. P. Boyce, the first President of SBTS, when he said:

> As a twenty-nine-year-old theology professor at Furman University, Boyce delivered his inaugural address as what became the Magna Carta of Southern Seminary, "Three Changes in Theological Institutions." … Boyce delivered his address as the ghost of Alexander Campbell still haunted the Baptist mind. Campbell criticized confessions of faith as assaults upon freedom of conscience and, as Boyce lamented, "threatened at one time the total destruction of our faith." As Boyce feared, "Had he occupied a chair in one of our theological institutions, that destruction might have been completed."[4]

I was recently asked at an SBC Church: How do you keep a denomination from sliding? The best answer I can come up with is that we must have a confession, actually believe that confession, and let it guide our cooperation and mission. History teaches us a consistent

---

2 Ibid 3-4.

3 The Campbellite movement shows up today primarily through Churches of Christ and Christian churches.

4 Dr. Albert Mohler's Inaugural Convocation Address at Southern Seminary in 1993, "Don't Just Do Something: Stand There." (Accessed 12/01/2022). https://equip.sbts.edu/resource/dont-just-do-something-stand-there/

lesson: you don't want to be on the side of the "no creed but the Bible" crowds, whether they be Campbellites, or the SBC theological liberals of years gone by. Our refusal to hold fast to and be guided by our confession certainly needed a "conservative resurgence." That's why our SBC entities, like our seminaries, required faculty to affirm the BFM2000.[5]

Confessions are a part of our history and must be a part of our future. They're also consistent with our Baptist distinctives. There seems to be a misconception floating around that holding to confessions for cooperation somehow violates local church autonomy. But this misconstrues what autonomy actually means. In one sense, autonomy means a church can decide to do whatever it desires according to its own collective conscience; it can govern itself how it deems best under the Lord. But autonomy and friendly cooperation aren't one and the same.

In fact, if they were, then churches could behave however they wanted and believe whatever they wanted and still be in "friendly cooperation" because, after all, they believe in "autonomy." The way some speak of autonomy essentially makes it the only distinctive for cooperation. If that were the case, then the only Baptist distinctive that would bind us together would be a commitment to a local church's absolute freedom of belief and practice. It's fairly obvious to conclude: such an arrangement would be a complete disaster. It would say to the world, "We are just about mission and not doctrine."

---

5 This is not just the case in Campbellite churches and the theological liberals of the SBC, but also among Northern Baptists. Check out Caleb Morell's article "A Confession Rejected and a Denomination Undone" - https://wng.org/opinions/a-confession-rejected-and-a-denomination-undone-1686225305)

That is — and has always been — a doomed project.[6] Churches that no longer believe or affirm a confession are free to do so (that is "autonomy"). But they are not free to do so and still demand to be a part of a confessional group (i.e. "friendly cooperation" in a free-church Convention).[7]

Confessions are a part of our Baptist history. They're important for various reasons, some of which have been mentioned here. That leads us to more fully consider how confessions have been used in the past.

---

6   In the summer of 2023, I tweeted about this very concern as I interacted with Rick Warren and his arguments against confessionalism. I tweeted, "The word 'mission' alone demands a doctrine that defines what mission is, and more importantly, what we hold out to sinners in that 'mission.' Warren says we have always been about a 'common mission,' not a common confession' but even in the preamble of the BFM2000 it says, 'Baptists are a people of deep beliefs and cherished doctrines. Throughout our history we have been a confessional people.' Second, being a convention demands we cooperate on "second tier" issues. Warren says, 'We have never demanded every Baptist agree on every interpretation.' This is true, but Baptists have certainly sought to distinguish themselves doctrinally, and a Statement of Faith is not equal to every interpretation." Please note that unrolled this thread for this quote, and I adapted the tweet to spell out full words that had been abbreviated in the original twitter thread: https://twitter.com/nateakin/status/1666536401284808705

7   As I tweeted in the summer of 2023: "Saddleback has hired females & called them 'pastor,' and they will continue to be able to do so regardless of what happens in NOLA. That is autonomy, but that is also outside the bounds of friendly cooperation w/ SBC faith and practice."

Chapter 3

BAPTIST CONFESSIONS (PART 2)

How have Baptist Confessions been used?

Confessions have been used for at least three purposes throughout Baptist History: 1) to express solidarity with other Christians coming out of the Reformation; 2) to express our distinctness as Baptists; and 3) to be a rallying point for cooperation in order to guard against error, heresy, and apathy concerning our distinctives.[8]

First, confessions are used to express our unity with broader, historic Christianity.

Confessions declare our unity with other orthodox Christians, particularly other Protestant traditions, on theological convictions such as the Five Solas of the Protestant Reformation. We see this with the 2nd London in which the authors intentionally adapted language

---

8 Baptist historian Robert Torbet makes the following observations regarding the use of confessions: 1) Maintain purity of doctrine 2) Clarify and validate the Baptist position 3) To serve as a guide to the General Assembly or local association in counseling churches 4) To serve as a basis for fellowship within associations 5) To discipline churches and members by withdrawing fellowship. Torbet, Robert. *A History of the Baptists* (3rd ed). The Judson Press, Valley Forge, PA, 46.

from the Presbyterians' Westminster Confession. They didn't do this because they were like me, a lazy high schooler who copied answers from my buddy before the beginning of class. No, they used similar language to intentionally show solidarity with other Protestants on what might be called first-tier doctrines: the nature of the Scriptures, the natures of Christ, the atonement, the bodily resurrection, etc. The framers of 2nd London said as much in the Preface:

> We did in like manner conclude it best to follow their example in making use of the very same words with them both, in these articles wherein our faith and doctrine is the same with theirs. And this we did, the more abundantly, to manifest our consent with both, in all the fundamental articles of the Christian Religion ... declaring before God, Angels, & Men, our hearty agreement with them, in that wholesome Protestant Doctrine, which with so clear evidence of Scriptures they have asserted.[9]

Second, confessions express our uniqueness or distinctives as Baptists, which particularly relate to our ecclesiological convictions.

Not only do confessions promote our unity with other Protestant Christians, they also systematize the distinct doctrines we hold most dear. Take, for instance, the Preamble to the First London Confession of 1644 (1st London) which states as the purpose:

> The Confession of Faith, of those churches which are commonly (though falsely) called anabaptists: presented to the view of all that fear God, to examine by the touchstone of the Word of Truth: As likewise for the taking off those aspersions which are frequently both in pulpit

---

9 Throughout we are retaining the original spelling of these confessions, such as the English used here in the 2nd London.

and print, (although unjustly) cast upon them…. We have therefore for the clearing of the truth we profess, that it may be at liberty, though we be in bonds, briefly published a confession of our faith.

The Preamble to the 2nd London gives a similar, humble explanation of why they produced what they call "our" confession of faith and why it differs from other Protestants when necessary:

In those things wherein we differ from others, we have exprest our selves with all candor and plainness that none might entertain jealousie of ought secretly lodged in our breasts, that we would not the world should be acquainted with; yet we hope we have also observed those rules of modesty, and humility, as will render our freedom in this respect inoffensive, even to those whose sentiments are different from ours. We have also taken care to affix texts of Scripture, in the margin for the confirmation of each article in our confession; in which work we have studiously indeavoured to select such as are most clear and pertinent, for the proof of what is asserted by us: and our earnest desire is, that all into whose hands this may come, would follow that (never enough commended) example of the noble Bereans, who searched the Scriptures daily, that they might find out whether the things preached to them were so or not.

The more recent BFM2000 demonstrates our desire to express what we call *the* Baptist faith and message we hope to share with the world. In later chapters, we'll unpack some of these distinctives.

Third, confessions act as a rallying point for cooperation and missions that seek to combat

heresy, error, apathy, and pragmatism.

Confessions act both as a rallying point and a boundary for cooperation. The signatories of the 2nd London stated it like this:

> We the Ministers, and Messengers of, and concerned for upwards of, one hundred Baptised Churches, in England and Wales (denying Arminianism), being met together in London, from the third of the seventh month to the eleventh of the same, 1689, to consider of some things that might be for the glory of God, and the good of these congregations, have thought meet (for the satisfaction of all other Christians that differ from us in the point of Baptism) to recommend to their perusal the confession of our faith, which confession we own, as containing the doctrine of our faith and practice, and do desire that the members of our churches respectively do furnish themselves therewith (Signatory Section).

As for Baptists in America, confessions have always been at the genesis of cooperative efforts like the Pillar Network. Consider the Philadelphia Association, which Baptists formed in 1707. This was the first such association on American soil; they adapted the 2nd London into a statement that became known as the Philadelphia Confession. In reality, it was simply a reprinting of the 2nd London with two articles added: "Of Singing Psalms" and "Laying on of Hands." As doctrinal disputes arose, they said the 2nd London was the "confession of faith set forth by the elders and brethren met in London, 1689, and owned by us." Baptist historian William Lumpkin writes of Benjamin Keach, the author of the Philadelphia Confession: "[he did] much to encourage the idea of connectionalism among the assemblies with which he worked in America."[1]

---

1 Lumpkin, William. *Baptist Confessions of Faith.* Judson Press, 348.

The Triennial Convention,[2] the national convention that eventually split into the Northern and Southern Baptist Conventions, used the Philadelphia Confession for its supported missionaries. After a few generations, they used the New Hampshire Confession (1833) to determine cooperation. Timothy George points out, "Each of the 293 'delegates,' as they were then called, who gathered in Augusta to organize the Southern Baptist Convention in 1845, belonged to congregations and associations which had adopted the Philadelphia/Charleston Confession of Faith as their own."[3]

Thomas Kidd also addresses this point while admitting the SBC didn't have a formal confession for its first 80 years. He writes,

This is true, but it is somewhat irrelevant since so many Baptist churches and associations already had confessions when the SBC was founded. All the delegates who formed the SBC in 1845 belonged to churches and/or associations that adhered to a confession of faith, usually either the Philadelphia Baptist Confession (1742) or the New Hampshire Confession (1833), the latter being arguably the most influential Baptist confession in American history.... As a denomination, the SBC has now affirmed a confession of faith (the BFM) for almost a hundred years, or the majority of the time it has existed.... It's hard to know what these confessions were used for, if not to identify a common set of beliefs and practices for denominational unity and boundaries. There's no clear mission if you don't have a clear set of beliefs.[4]

---

2 We will discuss the Triennial Convention in more detail in Chapter 10, a convention formed by Baptists to support the missionary work of people like Adoniram Judson.

3 George. *Baptist Confessions, Covenants, and Catechisms,* 11.

4 Thomas Kidd, "Confessions of Faith and the Baptist Tradition" accessed at https://www.thegospelcoalition.org/blogs/evangelical-history/confessions-of-faith-and-the-baptist-tradition/ on 12/12/2023.

Confessions define doctrinal parameters for cooperative efforts in missions, but they also help to combat heresy and error. For example, the 1925 Baptist Faith and Message (1925BFM) addressed new and popular heretical views associated with evolution. The preamble states:

> The present occasion for a reaffirmation of Christian fundamentals is the prevalence of naturalism in the modern teaching and preaching of religion. Christianity is supernatural in its origin and history. We repudiate every theory of religion which denies the supernatural elements in our faith. As introductory to the doctrinal articles, we recommend the adoption by the Convention of the following statement of the historic Baptist conception of the nature and function of confessions of faith in our religious and denominational life, believing that some such statement will clarify the atmosphere and remove some causes of misunderstanding, friction, and apprehension.

Almost forty years later, the 1963 Baptist Faith and Message (1963BFM) addressed errors arising in the SBC over the nature of Scripture. Almost forty years after that, the 2000BFM was updated to address shifting views on gender and sexuality — which seems ironic given our current debates.

Russell Reno, formerly a professor of moral theology at Creighton University, sums up the role of confessions as a testimony to unity, a statement of distinctness, and a guard against heresy. He writes:

> The impulse behind confessions of faith is doxological, the desire to speak the truth about God, to give voice to the beauty of holiness in the fullest possible sense. However, the particular forms that historical confessions take are shaped by confrontation. Their purpose is to respond to the spirit of the age by re-articulating in a pointed way the specific

content of Christianity so as to face new challenges as well as new forms of old challenges. As a result, formal confessions are characterized by pointed distinctions. They are exercises in drawing boundaries where the particular force of traditional Christian claims is sharpened to heighten the contrast between orthodoxy and heresy, between true belief and false belief…. As they shape our beliefs, confessions structure our identities.[5]

However, when it comes to our shared distinctives, there's a danger more present than heresy: apathy. Our confessions, if they're truly kept, help us fight this approaching danger. Consider the turnaround of the SBC. More specifically, consider the turnaround of our SBC seminaries. When Dr. Mohler, and my dad alongside him, took over leadership at Southern Seminary, they were stepping into an institution that had been dominated for decades by liberal theologians. My father met professors who outright rejected inerrancy, embraced open theism, denied the exclusivity of the gospel and penal substitution, questioned the historicity of the resurrection, and advocated for praying to God as "mother." He met professors who were pro-abortion, pro-homosexuality, and pro-female pastors.[6] They had inherited a faculty who held to the creed "no creed but the Bible." Amid this confusion, both in the SBC at large and our SBC seminaries in particular, Mohler preached his first ever convocation at SBTS in 1993. Here's what he said of the Abstract of Principles, the document which was supposed to guide this confessional institution:

---

5   Russell Reno, "At the Crossroads of Dogma," in Reclaiming the Faith, ed. Ephraim Radner and George R. Sumner. Grand Rapids: Eerdmans, 1993, 105.

6   For more examples of the theological liberalism check out Servant Songs by Randall Lolley for Southeastern Baptist Theological Seminary and "Once There was Camelot" by Susan Shaw and Tisa Lewis for The Southern Baptist Theological Seminary.

A denomination once marked by intense theological commitment and a demonstrable theological consensus has seen that doctrinal unity pass into a programmatic consciousness. We are in danger of losing our theological grammar, and, more seriously by far, of forfeiting our theological inheritance.... **As Southern Baptists, we are in danger of becoming God's most unembarrassed pragmatists much more enamored with statistics than invested in theological substance....** The Abstract represents a clarion call to start with conviction rather than mere action. It cries out, "Don't just do something, stand there!" ... In the view of eternity, we will be judged most closely, not on the basis of how many courses were taught, how many students were trained, how many syllabi were printed, or how many books were published, but on whether or not we kept the faith.[7]

And so Christians, let alone Baptists, have seen fit throughout the ages to take a stand on what they believe the Bible teaches. In doing so, they combat outright heresy and take clear stances amidst differing interpretations on key doctrines. To quote Boyce on why Southern Seminary needed a confession, "A crisis in Baptist Doctrine is evidently approaching, and those of us who still cling to the doctrines which formerly distinguished us, have the important duty to perform of earnestly contending for the faith once delivered to the saints. Gentleman, God will call us to judgment if we neglect it."[8]

This is why we believe it's important to be confessional. It's not because we're narrow-minded, but because we have a deposit that we're supposed to give to the world. We write these things down so we will not waiver with the winds of time. Sadly, many who have

---

7 Albert Mohler's Inaugural Convocation Address, "*Don't Just Do Something: Stand There!*"

8 James Petigru Boyce, "Three Changes in Theological Institutions: An Inaugural Address Delivered before the Board of Trustees of Furman University, the Night before the Annual Commencement, July 31, 1856," 15.

avoided confessions, like the Northern Baptists of America, have faded into oblivion. They've given in to overtly liberal theology, which has led to the death and decay of their own cooperation and mission efforts. So we must continue to write our confessions and hold on to them dearly, even as we long for the day when we will need them no longer! Of course, confessions aren't an end unto themselves. It's not enough to be confessional. We must also be convictional; we must actually believe and promote what our confessions state. If we are to "stand firm in the faith," then we must protect the doctrines that surround the gospel.

As we think about being convictional in our confessions, then it's a good time for us to consider how our Baptist distinctives protect the gospel and determine our ecclesiological convictions. We turn to those distinctives now.

Chapter 4

BAPTIST DISTINCTIVES

As I mentioned in the preface, I once had a crisis in which I wondered, "Am I really a Baptist?" As I dove into that question, I realized I was not alone. It seems for many that being a Baptist simply means being one who is in favor of dunking! Well, Baptists are certainly for believer's baptism by immersion, but there's much more to being a Baptist.

We now turn our attention to those distinctives.

A few things of note, however, before considering what might be called our Baptist distinctives:

First, there's not universal agreement on what constitutes Baptist distinctives. The old adage proves true: "Put two Baptists in a room and get three opinions." Nonetheless, there does seem to be at least a baseline of agreement. We'll give our attention to those that meet the most basic expectations.

Second, these distinctives are not unique to us. Agreeing with one of these distinctions doesn't make you a Baptist. It's agreeing to all of them — and agreeing to the reasons for believing in them — that makes you a Baptist. Baptists stand in a long line of orthodox, Protestant, Reformed Christianity. Yet even though we share first-tier agreements with many Christians, we disagree on how those first-tier agreements come to bear on our ecclesiological commitments, which I hope to demonstrate.

Third, we are people of the Book. Of course this conviction is not unique to Baptists. So we won't walk through that one. But the five we will consider arise out of a foundational affirmation of the inerrancy, authority, and sufficiency of the Word. In fact, biblical authority has been the first article of every major Baptist confession since the 2nd London Confession. In addition, our commitment not only to the Bible's inerrancy, but the straightforwardness of our hermeneutic leads us to doctrines like believer's baptism by immersion rather than paedobaptism. Put another way, if you just handed someone a Bible in a completely unreached people group without any knowledge of church history, then they would likely never come up with paedobaptism but rather a form of credobaptism.

Fourth, we are the rightful heirs of the Reformation. Because we emphasize the sufficiency of Scripture, and because the necessity of a regenerate membership more completely displays the Five Solas of the Reformation, it's not an exaggeration to say — a bit tongue-in-cheek — that Baptist theology completed what the Reformation began. Baptists have taken justification by faith alone to its proper end and application.

Chapter 5

REGENERATE CHURCH MEMBERSHIP

All five of our Baptist distinctives can be found in 1 Corinthians. We begin with regenerate church membership. We'll consider this topic biblically, historically, and practically.

Biblically

Most simply, a commitment to regenerate church membership means a commitment to a local church that is made up of born-again (converted) Christians. We see an emphasis on this doctrine as early as Acts 2:41–47. Luke points out that those who were saved were then baptized (more on this connection in the following chapter), and then he highlights how they belonged to the church:

> So those who received his word were baptized, **and there were added that day about three thousand souls.** And they devoted themselves to the apostles' teaching and **the fellowship**, to the breaking of bread and the prayers.... And all who believed were together and had all things in

common…. And day by day, attending the temple together and breaking bread in their homes, they received their food with glad and gener-
ous hearts, praising God and having favor with all the people. And the
Lord added to their number day by day those who were being saved
(Acts 2:41–42, 44–47). New believers were immediately brought into
the fellowship of faith that has come to be known as the first church, or
the church at Jerusalem. Passages like 1 Corinthians 12 highlight this
idea that every believer is considered a "member" of Christ's body, that
is, a local church.[1] The reverse also helps make the point. Unbelievers
are *not* united to Christ and thus not members of His body.

This Baptist distinctive may sound obvious, but as far back as
the patristic era, Augustine argues for a church made up of believers
and unbelievers, a *corpus permixtum*. For biblical support, he appeals
to the parable of the wheat and the tares. The field, he says, represents the church and so the church will be made up of believers and
unbelievers. Augustine's exegesis is problematic in part because the
text itself clearly states otherwise. Matthew writes, "Jesus answered,
'The one who sows the good seed is the Son of Man. **The field is
the world**, and the good seed is the sons of the kingdom. The weeds
are the sons of the evil one, and the enemy who sowed them is the
devil. The harvest is the end of the age, and the reapers are angels'"
(Matthew 13:37–39). It stands to reason that in the world there will
be believers and unbelievers, but it should not be so in the church —
nor is that what this parable teaches.[2]

Some say there's no prooftext for regenerate church membership, and that it is just assumed in the New Testament. But the

---

1 Also see Ephesians 4 and Romans 12.

2 Of course, at times, unbelievers who profess to be believers will make their way into the
church, but that is not an argument for abandoning this distinctive, but rather to care
about whom we admit as members and how we practice church discipline, another corol-
lary to this doctrine.

beginning of 1 Corinthians seems to exemplify this wonderful theological concept. Paul writes, "To the church of God that is in Corinth, **to those sanctified in Christ Jesus,** called to be **saints** together with all those who in every place **call upon the name of our Lord Jesus Christ**" (1 Corinthians 1:2). Paul calls them "the church of God" along with those who in every place call upon the name of our Lord Jesus Christ. Paul uses the phrase "church of God" in only one other place, when he tells the Ephesian elders in Acts 20:28 to care for the church of God "which He obtained by His own blood."

In addition, consider the staggering descriptions of Peter for the "elect exiles" in 1 Peter 2:9–10. "But you are a chosen race, a royal priesthood, a holy nation, a people for his own possession, that you may proclaim the excellencies of him who called you out of darkness into his marvelous light. Once you were not a people, but now you are God's people; once you had not received mercy, but now you have received mercy."

Finally, also consider Hebrews 8:10–12 which is quoting Jeremiah 31 to describe the newness of the New Covenant:

> "Behold, the days are coming, declares the Lord, when I will establish a new covenant with the house of Israel and with the house of Judah, not like the covenant that I made with their fathers on the day when I took them by the hand to bring them out of the land of Egypt. For they did not continue in my covenant, and so I showed no concern for them, declares the Lord. For this is the covenant that I will make with the house of Israel after those days, declares the Lord: I will put my laws into their minds, and write them on their hearts, and I will be their God, and they shall be my people. And they shall not teach, each one his neighbor and each one his brother, saying, 'Know the Lord,' for they shall all know me, from the least of them to the greatest. For I will be merciful toward their iniquities, and I will remember their sins no more."

In the New Covenant, those who are part of the people of God shall all know Him for they will have new hearts.

The church, then, isn't made up of those who aren't in Christ. It's not made up of those who cannot be called saints. It's not made up of those who cannot be called a people for His own possession, those who have been called out of darkness. It's not made up of those who cannot call on the name of Jesus, which is why infants cannot be counted as part of the Church.

It is not made up of those who do not know God. And it certainly isn't to be made up of those for whom the precious blood has not been applied!

If we take this Baptist distinctive seriously, then how will it change our membership processes? Amid that major city of Corinth, full of cultural influence and unrepentant sin, there existed a special people, a group of elect exiles set apart by God who were once "not a people, but now they are God's people." Amid that dark place stood an embassy of Christ's Kingdom, the church of God.

And these people have a job to do. They aren't supposed to just revel in what they've become, as wonderful as that is. They're supposed to go tell others what has happened to them. This set-apart people must proclaim his "excellencies" to the very ends of the earth.

Clearly, regenerate church membership isn't just a matter of soteriology but missiology.

Historically

Regenerate church membership has deep roots in Baptist history among theologians and in our confessions. I chose this distinctive first, even over believer's baptism, because I'm convinced they all spring out of this one. John Hammett calls regenerate church membership "the Baptist mark of the church."[1] A commitment to a regenerate church stood at the forefront of our breaking with other paedobaptist Protestants.

This has been a precious and important theological distinctive for our Baptist forebears. Benjamin Keach — one of the authors of the Philadelphia Confession, who was present at the 1689 Assembly that endorsed the 2nd London — wrote in 1697 a work called *The Glory of a True Church and its Discipline Display'd: Wherein a True Gospel-Church is Described Together with the Power of the Keys, and Who are to be Let In, and Who to be Shut Out*. The long title notwithstanding, the content is gold. He writes at the outset, "To the Baptized Churches, particularly to that under my Care. My Brethren, Every House or Building consisteth both of Matter and Form: And so doth the Church of Christ, or House of the Living God. The Matter or Materials with which it is built *are Lively Stones, i.e. Converted Persons*."[2] W.B. Johnson, the first SBC president, wrote the year after the forming of the SBC, "It is evident, that the materials of which the primitive churches were composed, were conscious subjects, who, upon profession of faith in Christ, were baptized in the name of the Father, and of the Son, and of the Holy Ghost. And as patterns for all succeeding churches, they should be imitated, since every church of Christ, throughout all time, should be composed of such materials as the primitive churches were composed of."[3] J.L. Reynolds, then the pastor of the Second Baptist Church of Richmond, Virginia, wrote in a work entitled *Church Polity or the Kingdom of Christ in its Internal and External Development*:

1 Hammett, John. *Biblical Foundations for Baptist Churches*. Kregel: Grand Rapids, MI. 81.

2 Dever. *Polity*. 9Marks Ministries: Washington D.C. 64. Emphasis mine.

3 Ibid. 180.

> Each particular Church seeks to represent, in itself, the kingdom of Christ, and ought, therefore, to be composed entirely of spiritual materials. It is no part of its design to embrace unbelievers, and prepare them for the kingdom of heaven. They have no right to its privileges and blessings. They are intruders at its ordinances. No ecclesiastical recognition of them as children, can change their relation as aliens and strangers; and they who introduce them contravene the declared will of the great Head of the Church. The gates of his kingdom are open to none but converted men. It is, therefore, the imperative duty of the Churches to admit to membership none but such as give satisfactory evidence that they have been born again. This was the practice of the apostles.[4]

This Baptist distinctive explains how our Baptist forebears viewed the church, both in this country and across the ocean. This observation bears itself out in our confessions as well.

Regenerate Church Membership in the Confessions:

First London

XXXIII. Jesus Christ hath here on earth a [manifestation of His] spiritual kingdom, which is His Church, whom He hath purchased *and redeemed* to Himself as a peculiar inheritance; which Church is *a company of visible saints, called and separated from the world by the word and Spirit of God, to the visible profession of faith of the gospel,* being baptized into that faith, and joined to the Lord, and each other, by mutual agreement in the practical enjoyment of the ordinances commanded by Christ their head and king.

---

4 Ibid. 323.

Somerset Confession of 1656

THAT in admitting of members into the church of Christ, it is the duty of the church, and ministers whom it concerns, in faithfulness to God, that they *be careful they receive none but such as do make forth evident demonstration of the new birth*, and the work of faith with power (John 3:3; Matt. 3:8, 9; Acts 8:37; Ezek. 44:6, 7, Acts 2:38; 2 Cor. 9:14; Ps. 26:4, 5; 101:7).

Second London

CHAP. XXVI. Of the Church. 1. The Catholic or universal Church, which (with respect to the internal work of the Spirit, and truth of grace) may be called invisible, *consists of the whole (a) number of the Elect*, that have been, are, or shall be gathered into one, under Christ the head thereof; and is the spouse, the body, the fulness of him that filleth all in all. a Heb. 12.23. Col. 1.18. Eph. 1.10,22.23. & ch. 5.23,27,32.2. All persons throughout the world, *professing the faith of the Gospel*, and obedience unto God by Christ, according unto it; not destroying their own profession by any Errors everting the foundation, or unholyness of conversation, (b) are and may be called *visible Saints; (c) and of such ought all particular Congregations to be constituted.*

New Hampshire

XIII. Of a Gospel Church. We believe that a visible church of Christ is *a congregation of baptized believers*, associated by covenant in the faith and fellowship of the gospel; observing the ordinances of Christ; governed by his laws; and exercising the gifts, rights, and privileges invested in them by his word; that its only scriptural officers are bishops or pastors and deacons whose qualifications, claims and duties are defined in the Epistles to Timothy and Titus. (**Note:**

Each version of the Baptist Faith and Message, 1925, 1963, 2000, has almost exact language to the New Hampshire).

Practical Applications

Finally, let us consider some practical applications and considerations. Being committed to regenerate church membership means we must be careful to bring into membership only those who, as Reynolds put it, "give satisfactory evidence that they have been born again." To discern this, we must have a formal, intentional membership process. The practice of some Baptist churches from the past, where one joined the church simply by walking the aisle at the end of the service, is clearly insufficient if we hold this commitment. One way to hold tightly to this concept is through a membership class and a pastoral interview with any potential member. It's important to make sure prospective members understand the gospel, first and foremost. It's also important that they understand the privileges and responsibilities of being a church member. Paul tells the Ephesians that the church "displays the manifold wisdom of God" (Eph. 3:10). That's why Paul and Peter go to such lengths to make sure we understand the true identity of those who make up the church. It's for their own good (that they understand their true condition), but it's also for the testimony and witness of the church that is supposed to put the glory of God on display for the world. It seems vital for us to hold dear this distinctive so that we can, in line with our Baptist fathers and the Apostles, help our churches more clearly display God's manifold wisdom.

Chapter 6

BELIEVER'S BAPTISM BY IMMERSION

The second Baptist distinctive is Believer's Baptism by Immersion.

This distinctive can be found in 1 Corinthians 12:12–14 as the radical act signifying our union to Jesus Christ and to his people. Almost all traditions (paedobaptist, Catholics, etc.) argue that Baptism is the entrance ordinance (or sacrament) into the church. It signifies who is a part of the people of God. So it's not necessarily that we Baptists disagree as to the place of baptism in the order of the ordinances, but we disagree in the timing and manner of who is to be baptized and how.

This distinctive flows out of regenerate church membership because we only give the entrance sign of the kingdom to those who are *in* the kingdom. Consider *who* and *how* one becomes part of the people of God and you'll begin to understand why credobaptism (or believer's baptism) is so important to us. It's not just some trivial difference. In the Old Covenant you usually "got in" by generation; in the

New Covenant, you "get in" by regeneration. In the Old Covenant, people got in by being born; in the New Covenant, you're only in once you're born again. Believer's baptism by immersion best depicts how *new* the New Covenant is. It validates members in that Covenant who have died with Christ, been buried, and raised to new life. The physical practice of believer's baptism is attested to in Acts, and spiritually unpacked in places like Romans 6 and 1 Corinthians 12.

Let's then consider biblical baptism. Baptism is the first command after the call to make disciples (Matt 28:19–20). Baptism is thus connected to the beginning of discipleship and to the church, as we saw in the previous chapter which highlighted a few textual connections to regenerate church membership (Matt 28:19–20; Acts 2:38–42). Biblical baptism can be helpfully understood, as others have put it, to include the right member, mode, meaning, and medium.

Right member: Baptism is for believers. Baptism is only for believers, those who have been born again (regenerated) and who are themselves members of the body of Christ. Baptism is always mentioned in connection with belief and/or union with Christ, which means we must not give the physical sign of baptism to someone who has not experienced the spiritual realities of what baptism portrays (Rom. 6 and 1 Cor. 12). This has implications for paedobaptists, but also for those in Baptist circles who too often practice what amounts to toddler baptism, i.e., baptizing someone who can't articulate the gospel or their conversion in any meaningful sense. (For reference: Matt 28:19–20; Acts 2:38–42; 8:34–39; 9:17–19; 10:44–48; 16:14–15, 33–34; 18:8; Rom 6:1–10; 1 Cor 12:13; Gal 3:27; Col 2:12; 1 Pet 3:21–22).

Right mode: Baptism isn't *by* immersion; Baptism *is* immersion. The English word "baptism" comes from a transliterated form of the Greek word "baptizo," which means to immerse or dip. In fact, we wouldn't even have the word "baptism" if King James translators had just translated the word as it should have been translated. They chose not to do this, however, perhaps because of their common practice of paedobaptism. So they made up a word: "baptize." Immersion, however, is the biblical and appropriate mode because baptism depicts our union with Christ, that we have died to sin, been buried (completely cut off in a watery grave), and raised to new life in Christ (Rom 6:1–10). Jesus Himself provided an example for baptism by immersion during His time on earth (Matt 3:13–17).[1] So we don't just differ with our paedobaptist brothers and sisters because of what the word means but also because of what the act of baptism itself depicts.

Right meaning: Baptism is a physical picture of what has happened to us spiritually. It's necessary to distinguish that it is not salvific but is rather a picture of one's salvation. Although some use texts like Acts 2:38 to push for what is called "baptismal regeneration," where the act of baptism by itself saves a person, the Book of Acts on its own terms is replete with examples of people who were saved apart from baptism. In addition, the notion of baptismal regeneration completely does away with justification by faith alone and is upended by texts like Romans 10 that help us to see that confession with our mouth and heart save.

Right medium: Baptism is given to the church and should be done by the church or at the outset of the formation of a church (Acts 2:38–42; 8:34–39). Baptism shouldn't happen outside of that

---

1 A point where John Calvin and Martin Luther agree. Luther states, "For this reason I would have those who are to be baptized completely immersed in the water, as the word says… And this is doubtless the way in which it was instituted by Christ." *The Babylonian Captivity of the Church.* Fortress Press: Minneapolis, MN. 191. Calvin writes, "It is evident that the term 'baptize' means to immerse, and that this was the form used by the primitive Church." (*Institutes*, IV.15.19)

context. Since baptism is placed at the beginning of discipleship in Matthew 28:19–20, and since it doubles as the entrance to the Church in Acts 2:38–42, it has a key role both in discipleship and membership in the local church.

Baptism is important because of what it communicates to the church, to the one being baptized, and to the world. Through believer's baptism, we take the *solas* of the Reformation to their appropriate place.[2] John MacArthur pointed this out more than two decades ago in his debate with his friend R.C. Sproul: paedo-baptism only brings confusion to justification by faith alone. In an extended but powerful quote, MacArthur explains why paedobaptism brings confusion whereas credobaptism upholds justification by faith alone.

> Because there is no faith in the child, there is no comprehension of the gospel, there is no repentance in the child.... And they talk about, "Well you have sort of a peremptory election act, or you have a peremptory salvation act in the child." You can read the strangest kind of statements that are made. I wrote down about 25 different statements from books I read on what the baptism of an infant meant, and they were all varying shades of all kinds of things, but all agreeing that it didn't save but it put them in some place where they were more fortunate and likely to be more blessed by God. And I say that's no different place than any child would have, baptized or unbaptized living in a godly environment.... It is a needless thing to do because it ministers no saving grace to the child, it guarantees no future salvation to the child. And on the other hand, it perpetuates a misconception in the mind of parents that against all evidence, this child is somehow saved because of some event that occurred at their baptism. Luther had to go so far as to finally say they have

---

2 Five Solas: Salvation by grace alone, through faith alone, in Christ alone, to the Glory of God alone known by Scripture alone.

unconscious faith because he knew salvation was by faith. Children are children, they do not understand. I cannot for the life of me understand why you'd want the convolute the purity and the clarity of the doctrine of justification by grace through faith alone to the one who comes and repents of sin and embraces Jesus Christ with this act which admittedly has no saving efficacy, delivers no redeeming grace, infers no faith, is not symbolic of any union with Christ. The only point of it is to confound the person about what this meant and to confound the church with an unregenerate membership.… . The confusion in Christendom would be greatly lessened. The church would be instantly purged. Christ would be honored if there weren't millions of people outside salvation running around with a false security and bearing an untrue symbol of an unreal condition. I really feel that we Reformed folks need to finish the Reformation here and I see this as a way to do that. Two ways are before us. I really believe one embodies ritualism, institutional church mixed with the saved and lost… . The other leads to faith alone, the glory of the cross and resurrection and the true identity of the redeemed church. Baptism is at the crossroads. The cry of the Reformation was not tradition, tradition, tradition … the fathers, the fathers, the fathers … but Scripture, Scripture, Scripture.[3]

Historically

Baptists across centuries and contexts have held strongly to this conviction. Consider the following quote from the great British Baptist Andrew Fuller, the key theologian of the modern mission movement. He delivered a sermon on his own confession of faith as he was being installed as the new pastor at First Baptist Church at Kettering, on October 7, 1783. Here's what he said about baptism:

3 John MacArthur, *"The Case for Believer's Baptism: The Credo Baptist Position"* https://www.gty.org/library/articles/A360/case-for-believers-baptism-the-credo-baptist-position (accessed Dec. 21, 2023).

I believe, the ordinances which Christ, as King of Zion, has instituted for his church to be found in, throughout the gospel day, are especially two: namely, Baptism and the Lord's Supper. **I believe the subjects of both to be those who profess repentance towards God, and faith towards our Lord Jesus Christ;** and on such I consider them as incumbent duties. I believe that it is essential to Christian baptism, **that it be by immersion**, or burying the person in water, in the name of the Father, the Son, and the Holy Ghost. I likewise believe baptism as administered by the primitive church, to be prerequisite to church communion; hence I judge what is called strict communion to be consistent with the word of God.[4]

On American soil, theologian John Dagg gave a copious defense of believer's baptism by immersion in his *Manual on Church Polity*. He spends two chapters (nearly 120 pages in my copy) dismantling a number of objections to credobaptism. Dagg not only takes on the matter biblically and theologically, but historically traces the emergence of the error known as paedobaptism. Dagg writes:

No trace of infant baptism can be found, previous to the time of Justin Martyr... the late Neander, who is esteemed the greatest of ecclesiastical historians, says: "Baptism was administered at first only to adults, as men were accustomed to conceive baptism and faith as strictly connected. Immediately after Irenaeus, in the last years of the second century, Tertullian appears as a zealous opponent of infant baptism: a proof that the practice had not as yet come to be regarded as an apostolical institution." ... Jacobi, a learned friend of Neander, says: "Infant baptism

---

4 Andrew Fuller's Ordination Sermon: http://baptisthistoryhomepage.com/fuller. andrw.conf.of.fath.html (accessed Dec. 21, 2023).

was established neither by Christ nor the apostles. Many circumstances conspired early to introduce the practice of infant baptism."[5]

We could turn to other Baptist theologians, but it will be helpful to see again how we have spoken of believer's baptism by immersion in our confessions.

1st London:

XXXIX. Baptism is an ordinance of the New Testament, given by Christ, *to be dispensed upon persons professing faith,* or that are made disciples; who upon profession of faith, ought to be baptized, and after to partake of the Lord's Supper. Matt. 28:18,19; John 4:1; Mark 16:15,16; Acts 2:37,38, 8:36,37, etc.

XL. *That the way and manner of dispensing this ordinance, is dipping or plunging the body under water;* it being a sign, must answer the things signified, which is, that interest the saints have in the death, burial, and resurrection of Christ: And that as certainly as the body is buried under water, and risen again, so certainly shall the bodies of the saints be raised by the power of Christ, in the day of the resurrection, to reign with Christ. Matt. 3:16; Mark 15:9 reads (into Jordan) in Greek; John 3:23, Acts 8:38; Rev. 1:5, 7:14; Heb. 10:22; Rom. 6:3,4,5,6; 1 Cor. 15:28,29. The word *baptizo* signifies to dip or plunge (yet so as convenient garments be both upon the administrator and subject with all modesty).

2nd London:

CHAP. XXIX. Of Baptism. Baptism is an Ordinance of the New Testament, ordained by Jesus Christ, to be unto the party Baptized, *a sign of his fellowship with him,* in his death, (c) and

---

5 Dagg, John. *Manual of Church Order.* 200-201.

resurrection; of his being engrafted into him; of (d) remission of sins; and of his (e) giving up unto God through Jesus Christ to live and walk in newness of Life. c Rom. 6.3,4,5. Col. 2.12. Gal. 3.27. d Mar. 1.4. Act. 26.16. [Note] e Rom, 6.2,4. 2. *Those who do actually professe (f) repentance towards God, faith in, and obedience, to our Lord Jesus, are the only proper subjects of this ordinance.* f Mar. 16.16. Act. 8.36,37. 3. The outward element to be used in this ordinance (g) is water, wherein the party is to be baptized, in the name of the Father, and of the Son, and of the Holy Spirit. g Mat 28.19,20. with Act. 8.38.4. *Immersion or dipping of the person (h) in water, is necessary to the due administration of this ordinance.* h Mat. 3.16. Joh. 3.23.

New Hampshire:

XIV. Of Baptism and the Lord's Supper. We believe that the Christian baptism *is the immersion in water of a believer,* into the name of the Father, and Son, and Holy Ghost; to show forth in a solemn and beautiful emblem, our faith in the crucified, buried and risen Saviour, with its effect, in our death to sin and resurrection to a new life; that *it is prerequisite to the privileges of a church relation,* and to the Lord's Supper; in which the members of the church by the sacred use of bread and wine, are to commemorate together the dying love of Christ; preceded always by solemn self-examination. Acts 8:36-39; Matt. 3:5–6; John 3:22–23; John 4:12; Matt. 28:19–20; Mark 16:16; Acts 2:38; Acts 8:12; Acts 16:32-34; Acts 18:8; Acts 10:47–48; Gal.3:26–28; Rom. 6:4; Col. 2:12; I Peter 3:20–21; Acts 22:16; Acts 2:41–42; 1 Cor. 11:26; Matt. 26:26–29; Mark 14:22–25; Luke 22:14–20; 1 Cor. 11:28; 1 Cor. 5:1–8; 1 Cor. 10:3–32; 1 Cor. 11:17–32; John 6:26.

BFM2000:

VII. Baptism and the Lord's Supper

Christian baptism is the immersion of a believer in water in the name of the Father, the Son, and the Holy Spirit. It is an act of obedience symbolizing the believer's faith in a crucified, buried, and risen Saviour, the believer's death to sin, the burial of the old life, and the resurrection to walk in newness of life in Christ Jesus. It is a testimony to his faith in the final resurrection of the dead. Being a church ordinance, *it is prerequisite to the privileges of church membership* and to the Lord's Supper.

Practical Applications:

There's much that could be said here, but at minimum we should make sure we only baptize believers and that we do so by immersion. We should thoroughly interview all baptismal candidates to ascertain whether they are in the faith. In addition, baptism should be connected to membership in the local church. We could also conduct classes on baptism to help candidates understand the ordinance and allow the church to examine the candidate's confession. When someone professes faith, we should move slowly on baptism, resisting the urge to spontaneously or immediately baptize all who profess faith in Christ.[6]

---

6 Our commitments to a regenerate church membership, believer's baptism, and the connection of baptism and membership, historically, has left us to delay baptism. There is an emergence of those who push for what is labeled "spontaneous baptism" as "the" biblical position, yet there is good reason to push back on this claim and to understand why Baptists have historically not practiced such baptismal practices. For more on this, check out John Hammett's article "What's the Rush?" published at the International Mission Board website: https://www.imb.org/2018/04/05/immediate-baptism-missions/

Conclusion

What a precious sign Christ has given His church to signify their death to sin, resurrection to eternal life, and union with one another. We dare not practice this sign flippantly. Our brothers and sisters in previous generations have died or been persecuted for believing so strongly in believer's baptism.[7] May we also be found faithful with this radical act demonstrating in Christ that we have already been through the waters of Jordan and are now home in the Promised Land!

---

[7] See Timothy George's article *"Believer's Baptism"* in Modern Reformation, Aug. 6, 2007. He writes, "This was a radical act in England in the 1640s. Thomas Edwards, Presbyterian polemicist, was greatly shocked at this practice of believers' Baptism by immersion. In one of his writings he issued the following: 'Whosoever re-baptized any that had been formerly baptized should be immediately cast into the water and drowned.' As a matter of fact, few if any English Baptists were drowned in the seventeenth century, unlike the Anabaptists on the continent in an earlier period. However, since their meetings were illegal, many of them spent time in prison and some died there during the years of persecution prior to the Act of Toleration of 1689." (https://www.modernreformation.org/resources/articles/believers-baptism, accessed Mar. 15, 2023).

Chapter 7

LOCALLY AUTONOMOUS AND ELDER-LED CONGREGATIONALISM

A third Baptist distinctive is what one might call locally autonomous, elder-led Congregationalism. The title is a bit clunky, but
these things go together. This distinctive also flows out of a regenerate, believers-only church. We find congregationalism throughout 1
Corinthians, particularly as the text pertains to discipline and various responsibilities. Since we are regenerate members who have the
Spirit, we can and must be responsible, accountable, and meaningful
participants in the work of the kingdom through the local church.
Since we are part of the kingdom through our re-birth, we all, as
a kingdom of priests, have been collectively given the keys of the
kingdom. Every member of Christ's church — not just its elders or
leaders — has the responsibility to determine who is in and out of
the church, who leads the church, and what the church believes.

This distinctive deals with church polity, or how a church is to be governed. ***Therefore, the most biblically faithful church polity is best described as a local, autonomous church that is Jesus-Designed, Elder-Led, Deacon-Served, and Congregationally Ruled.*** It is Jesus-designed because Jesus is the one who builds His church and He does so according to His Word. He is the architect (Matthew 16), and He gets to say how His church looks, runs, and is governed.

A Jesus-designed church is elder-led and deacon-served. Elders lead, which is why we are told in Hebrews 13:17, "Obey your leaders and submit to them, for they are keeping watch over your souls, as those who will have to give an account. Let them do this with joy and not with groaning, for that would be of no advantage to you." This is why Paul writes in 1 Thessalonians 5:12, "We ask you, brothers, to respect those who labor among you and are over you in the Lord and admonish you, and to esteem them very highly in love because of their work. Be at peace among yourselves."

In recent Southern Baptist life, there's been confusion over whether "elders," "bishops," and "pastors" refer to the same office. The BFM2000 is clear. These terms are distinct but synonymous. They describe different roles of elders: leading and shepherding. Pastors shepherd the sheep. Bishops provide spiritual oversight. An elder is a man of authority because of his character and ability to teach the Word so that those under his care flourish and are protected.

The Scriptures also speak of a second office in the church called deacons. Deacons serve the church so that the leaders can give their attention to the ministry of the Word and prayer (Acts 6, 1 Timothy 3). This is a helpful distinction I've heard from some: elders/pastors are a church's servant-leaders while deacons are its leading servants.

This brings us to the aspect of our polity that is most distinctly Baptist: *congregationalism*. Congregationalism means that the authority to decide a church's members, leaders, and doctrine resides within a church's members. Churches are autonomous, which means no extra-local body — a presbytery, a synod, a General Assembly, a Convention, or any broader denominational structure — can wield authority within a local congregation. The final authority for a church's members, leaders, and doctrines doesn't rest with a regional bishop or a Pope, but within the church's members. The New Testament demonstrates this claim several times. But for our purposes, we'll look at Acts 15, a contentious passage that other traditions and denominations appeal to in favor of a hierarchical structure.[1]

First, it's important to note that the church at Antioch initiates the meeting that becomes the Jerusalem Council. Because they were being badgered by men from Judea about being circumcised, Luke writes, "Paul and Barnabas and some of the others were appointed to go up to Jerusalem to the apostles and the elders about this question. So, being sent on their way by the church (Antioch) ..." (Acts 15:2b–3a).

Second, the final decision of the Jerusalem Council is made by the whole church, not just the apostles or elders (nor for future purposes with bishops or popes).[2] Notice what Luke records: "Then it seemed good to the apostles and the elders, with the whole church" (Acts 15:22a).

Third, if the Acts 15 passage is meant to describe a binding hierarchical system, then it's surprising that nowhere in the New Testament are we given instructions on creating such a structure. All of this develops later on but we find little-to-no support for it in the

---

1 The confessions and the theologians we examine later in the chapter will address points of Scripture that also highlight the autonomy of the churches in the New Testament.

2 It is clear in the New Testament that the term bishop is synonymous with elder and does not have an oversight role over other elders since the Ephesian elders are also called bishops, as are the elders in 1 Peter 5.

Scriptures. It's worth noting that the act of expanding beyond the New Testament offices of elder and deacon arose in the 2nd century when Ignatius of Antioch introduced a third office of bishop, who ruled above elders and deacons. The earlier *Didache* argues for only two offices of elder and deacon.[3] This is not to say that denominations or networks that spur cooperation are unbiblical. Of course they aren't! But they should only exist insofar as they help local churches accomplish their kingdom purposes.

Where does the New Testament teach the autonomy of the local church and its authority in matters of membership, leadership, and doctrine? We'll now answer that question. For a recap, congregationalism asserts that the gathered congregation of regenerate members have been given the keys to the kingdom in matters of membership (Matt. 18, 1 Cor. 5, 2 Cor. 2), leadership (Acts 6, 1 Tim. 5), and doctrine (Acts 15, Gal. 1).

The Entrance and Exit of Membership

God has given the keys of the kingdom to the congregation. Consider first Matthew 16 and 18. Matthew 16:15–20 states:

> He said to them, "But who do you say that I am?" Simon Peter replied, "You are the Christ, the Son of the living God." And Jesus answered him, "Blessed are you, Simon Bar-Jonah! For flesh and blood has not revealed this to you, but my Father who is in heaven. **And I tell you, you are Peter, and on this rock I will build my church, and the gates of hell shall not prevail against it. I will give you the keys of the kingdom of heaven, and whatever you bind on earth shall be bound in heaven, and whatever you loose on earth shall be loosed in heaven."**

3 See Phil Newton's *Elders in the Life of the Church*, Kregel: Grand Rapids, 46.

Then he strictly charged the disciples to tell no one that he was the Christ.

Then, in Matthew 18:15–20, Jesus gives us more details to fill in our congregationalism, explaining how it's exercised through church discipline:

If your brother sins against you, go and tell him his fault, between you and him alone. If he listens to you, you have gained your brother. But if he does not listen, take one or two others along with you, that every charge may be established by the evidence of two or three witnesses. **If he refuses to listen to them, tell it to the church.** And if he refuses to listen even to the church, let him be to you as a Gentile and a tax collector. **Truly, I say to you, whatever you bind on earth shall be bound in heaven, and whatever you loose on earth shall be loosed in heaven.** Again I say to you, if two of you agree on earth about anything they ask, it will be done for them by my Father in heaven. For where two or three are gathered in my name, there am I among them.

From these two texts, we can deduce that it is the role of the gathering (ἐκκλησία, *ekklesia*) to fence both the entrance and exit of the local church.

Later in the New Testament, 1 Corinthians builds on this concept. Paul writes in 1 Corinthians 5:1–5:

It is actually reported that there is sexual immorality among you, and of a kind that is not tolerated even among pagans, for a man has his father's wife. And you are arrogant! Ought you not rather to mourn? Let him who has done this be removed from among you. For though absent in body, I am present in spirit; and as if present, I have already pronounced judgment on the one who did such a thing. When you are assembled in the name of the Lord Jesus and my spirit is present, with the power of our Lord Jesus, you are to deliver this man to Satan for the destruction of the flesh, so that his spirit may be saved in the day of the Lord.

It's important to remember that this letter is written to the "church of God in Corinth." In fact, elders or deacons are never mentioned in 1 Corinthians. However, 1 Corinthians continues to emphasize the role of church members. Paul continues,

> For what have I to do with judging outsiders? **Is it not those inside the church whom you are to judge?** God judges those outside. "Purge the evil person from among you." When one of you has a grievance against another, does he dare go to law before the unrighteous instead of the saints? **Or do you not know that the saints will judge the world? And if the world is to be judged by you, are you incompetent to try trivial cases? Do you not know that we are to judge angels?** How much more, then, matters pertaining to this life! So if you have such cases, why do you lay them before those who have no standing in the church? I say this to your shame. Can it be that there is no one among you wise enough to settle a dispute between the brothers, but brother goes to law against brother, and that before unbelievers? To have lawsuits at all with one another is already a defeat for you. Why not rather suffer wrong? Why not rather be defrauded? But you yourselves wrong and defraud — even your own brothers (1 Cor. 5:12–6:8)!

Paul highlights the significant role of members in the life of the church and their future role in judging angels.[4] God has given the

---

4   In examining 1 Corinthians 6, it needs to be highlighted that Paul has in mind here matters of church discipline and financial disputes, not criminal acts. Criminal acts are matters for the State which wields the sword against evildoers according to Romans 13.

church the keys to guard who is in and out. This is not small matter; it really is a matter of the glory of God, the witness of the church, and the health of the body. We see in 1 Corinthians 5 that church discipline is also for the good of the one disciplined ("that his spirit may be saved in the day of our Lord").

We need to realize just how radical and important it is to be a member of a local church. God has set the boundaries of who is a part of the church (Spirit-indwelt saints). Amazingly, he tasks those same saints to fence the community of faith that bears witness about Him to the world. They also have the responsibility to restore the erring member provided he repents. Paul writes in his second letter to the Corinthians, "Now if anyone has caused pain, he has caused it not to me, but in some measure — not to put it too severely — to all of you. For such a one, this punishment by the majority is enough, so you should rather turn to forgive and comfort him, or he may be overwhelmed by excessive sorrow" (2 Corinthians 2:5–7).[5]

Leadership Affirmation

Acts 6 provides one key passage to help us see the congregation's role in affirming leaders. In this case, the Jerusalem church appoints deacons (or proto-deacons) to serve the church in making sure the Hellenistic widows were getting food. In doing so, they free up the apostles for the ministry of the Word and prayer. Luke records:

> Now in these days when the disciples were increasing in number, a com-
> plaint by the Hellenists arose against the Hebrews because their wid-
> ows were being neglected in the daily distribution. And the twelve sum-
> moned the full number of the disciples and said, "It is not right that we

---

5 This passage is one such text that leads Congregationalists to vote on congregational matters so that "the majority" may be established.

should give up preaching the word of God to serve tables. **Therefore, brothers, pick out from among you seven men of good repute, full of the Spirit and of wisdom, whom we will appoint to this duty.** But we will devote ourselves to prayer and to the ministry of the word." And what they said pleased the whole gathering, and they chose Stephen, a man full of faith and of the Holy Spirit, and Philip, and Prochorus, and Nicanor, and Timon, and Parmenas, and Nicolaus, a proselyte of Antioch. These they set before the apostles, and they prayed and laid their hands on them (Acts 6:1–6).

As this problem arose, the church was to "pick out from among" themselves men who were of "good repute, full of the Spirit and of wisdom." These were to be men of character, very much keeping in line with how Paul talks about deacons as he establishes their qualifications in 1 Timothy 3:8–13.

Another key passage on congregationalism pertains to the church's authority over its elders/pastors. We are given clear details as to how the church ought to hold elders accountable when they're guilty of public, persistent sin, which includes how to remove them from office. Paul explains the process in 1 Timothy 5:19–22:

Do not admit a charge against an elder except on the evidence of two or three witnesses. As for those who persist in sin, rebuke them in the presence of all, so that the rest may stand in fear. In the presence of God and of Christ Jesus and of the elect angels I charge you to keep these rules without prejudging, doing nothing from partiality. Do not be hasty in the laying on of hands, nor take part in the sins of others; keep yourself pure.

Paul instructs Timothy how the congregation should handle the potential exit of a pastor. The same logic holds true for membership;

if the congregation holds the keys to remove a pastor for unrepentant sin, then they also hold the keys for affirming a man into the office. This raises a theological and even practical implication which supports congregationalism. No one is a pastor because they assert it by themselves. A pastor is a pastor if and only if he has a flock willing to follow him.

From this, we get our concept of "derived authority." The pastor/elder's authority is ultimately from God Himself who allows him to lead, but it is also derived from the congregation who willingly submits to him. In one sense, every single church is congregational. Even if they don't have the formal right to vote a pastor out, they have the option to remove themselves out from under his authority by leaving that church. A pastor/elder can only hold the office if he aspires, is qualified, *and* is affirmed by a particular church.

Two more key passages make congregationalism, rather than hierarchical structure, clear. It seems like the whole congregation sets apart, sends, and receives back Barnabas and Paul for their first missionary journey. Luke records:

Now there were **in the church** at Antioch prophets and teachers, Barnabas, Simeon who was called Niger, Lucius of Cyrene, Manaen a lifelong friend of Herod the tetrarch, and Saul. **While they were worshiping** the Lord and fasting, the Holy Spirit said, "Set apart for me Barnabas and Saul for the work to which I have called them." Then after fasting and praying **they laid their hands on them and sent them off...** .

Then they passed through Pisidia and came to Pamphylia. And when they had spoken the word in Perga, they went down to Attalia, and from there they sailed to Antioch, where they had been commended to the grace of God for the work that they had fulfilled. And when they arrived and gathered the church together, they declared all that God had done with them, and how he had opened a door of faith to the Gentiles. And they remained no little time with the disciples (Acts 13:1–3, 14:24–28).

Scholars such as John Stott and John Polhill argue that the whole church is in mind in the gathering at the beginning of Acts 13.[6] This makes sense because when Paul and Barnabas return the whole church receives them back. It takes the intentional action of apostles, along with the whole church of Antioch, in order to send the church's first missionaries. This is similar to what we see in Acts 15 at the Jerusalem Council. In addition, it appears local churches also appointed a messenger, who many think is Apollos, for the carrying of a gift, or "act of grace" for the churches. Paul records, "With him we are sending the brother who is famous among all the churches for his preaching of the gospel. And not only that, but **he has been appointed by the churches** to travel with us as we carry out this act of grace that is being ministered by us, for the glory of the Lord himself and to show our good will" (2 Corinthians 8:18-19). The brother "famous among all the churches for his preaching of the gospel" is "appointed" by the churches for this task. The word "*appointed*" is the same word used in Acts 14:23 when Paul appoints elders in the first church plants. Even for a task such as ministering, Apollos is sent and appointed by local churches.

Doctrine

Finally, it appears congregations are accountable for doctrine. Paul and Jesus hold the church responsible for erring doctrine. As Paul writes to the churches of Galatia, "I am astonished that you are so

---

6　Polhill writes, "In v. 2 'they' likely refers to the entire Antioch congregation gathered for worship," *Acts*. Broadman & Holman Publishers: Nashville, 290.

quickly deserting him who called you in the grace of Christ and are turning to a different gospel — not that there is another one, but there are some who trouble you and want to distort the gospel of Christ" (Galatians 1:6–7).

In addition, Jesus writes seven letters to churches in the book of Revelation and speaks to them about their own lamentable slide away from doctrinal accountability. It seems clear that local congregations — such as Ephesus, Smyrna, Pergamum, Thyatira, Sardis, Philadelphia, and Laodicea — are held accountable for how they keep the faith and hold close to the doctrine delivered to the churches.

History and Confessions

Once again, confessions on both sides of the Pond have demonstrated a commitment to this Baptist distinctive.[7] Consider this lengthy passage from Benjamin Keach's *The Glory of a True Church and Its Discipline Display'd* that highlights both the autonomous congregation's role in the entrance and exit of members, as well as the selection of leaders. Keach writes,

> The Power of the Keys, or to receive in and shut out of the Congregation, is committed unto the Church…
>
> 1.   The Church essential is the first Subject of the Keys.
> 2.   They must of necessity to their Preservation, purge themselves from all pernicious Members.
> 3.   They have Power to organize themselves with Officers. Yet I humbly conceive I may add, that the Concurrence of the Presbytery is needful hereunto.

---

7 For a more thorough look at various Baptist theologians and their contributions on congregationalism consider Mark Dever's book *Polity*.

4.   If need be that they call an Officer from without, or one of another Church, they must first admit him a Member, that they may ordain their Officer from among themselves.

5.   They have Power to reject a scandalous Pastor from Office and Membership.

This Power of Christ is exerted as committed to them by the Hands of the Elder appointed by Christ, the due management whereof is in and with the Church to be his Care and Trust, as a Steward, whereof he is accountable to Christ and the Church, not lording it over God's Heritage. And that the Power of the Keys is in the Church, appears to me from Matt. 18.

"If he will not hear the Church;" it is not said, if he will not hear the Elder, or Elders. As also that of the Apostle, in directing the Church to cast out the Incestuous Person, he doth not give this Counsel to the Elder or Elders of the Church, but to the Church; so he commands the Church to withdraw from every Brother that walks disorderly. "Purge out the old Leaven, that you may be a new Lump."[8]

In the United States, the first President of the Southern Baptist Convention, W. B. Johnson wrote about congregationalism in his work *The Gospel Developed*. Johnson highlights the autonomy and authority of the congregation:

The government of a church is sometimes called democratical, that is, a government by the members of the body. And so far as the mode of administering the laws of Christ is regarded, this is a proper term. For in the account given of the first churches, each one managed its own affairs within itself, by the voice of its own members, not amenable to any other church or body of churches. This appears in the Acts of

8   Dever, *Polity*. 71.

the Apostles, and their epistles to the churches. Take for example, the command of Paul to the Corinthian church, to put away the incestuous man. This act was done, as we learn for the following passage, by a majority, "sufficient to such a man is the punishment which was inflicted of many." ... And when the Corinthian church and the seven churches of Asia, that were in disorder, were addressed, they were addressed as distinct bodies, and directed to put away their own errors, without any intimation that if they did not, a council formed of delegates from any given number of churches, should interpose for the purpose. The government, then, of the first churches was democratical, purely so, as far as the application of the laws of Christ is considered, in the exercise of a popular vote by the members.[9]

Again, not only do the Baptist theologians write about such things, but the churches also codify them in their confessions.

First London

XXXVI. Being thus joined, **every [local] church hath power given them from Christ, for their wellbeing, to choose among themselves meet persons for elders and deacons, being qualified according to the word**, as those which Christ hath appointed in His testament, for the feeding, governing, serving, and building up of His Church; and that none have any power to impose on them either these or any other. Acts 1:23,26, 6:3, 15:22,25; Rom. 12:7,8; 1 Tim. 3:2,6,7; 1 Cor. 12:8,28; Heb. 13:7,17; 1 Pet. 5:1,2,3, 4:15.

XLII. Christ hath likewise given power to His Church to receive in, and cast out, any member that deserves it; and this power is given to every congregation, and not to one particular person, either member or officer, but in relation to the whole body,

---

in reference to their faith and fellowship. Rom. 15:2; Matt. 18:17; 1 Cor. 5:4,11,14, 12:6, 2:3; 2 Cor. 2:6,7.

Second London
CHAP. XXVI. Of the Church.

8. A particular Church gathered, and compleatly Organized, according to the mind of Christ, consists of Officers, and Members; **And the Officers appointed by Christ to be chosen and set apart by the Church** (so called and gathered) for the peculiar Administration of Ordinances, and Execution of Power, or Duty, which he intrusts them with, or calls them to, to be continued to the end of the World are (p) Bishops or Elders and Deacons.

12. As all Believers are bound to join themselves to particular Churches, when and where they have opportunity so to do; So all that are admitted unto the privileges of a Church, are also (b) **under the Censures and Government thereof**, according to the Rule of Christ.

New Hampshire XIII. Of a Gospel Church. We believe that a visible church of Christ is a congregation of baptized believers, associated by covenant in the faith and fellowship of the gospel; observing the ordinances of Christ; governed by his laws; **and exercising the gifts, rights, and privileges invested in them by his word**; that its only scriptural officers are bishops or pastors and deacons whose qualifications, claims and duties are defined in the Epistles to Timothy and Titus. 1 Cor. 1:1–3; Matt. 18:17; Acts 5:11; Acts 8:1; Acts 11:21–23; 1 Cor. 4:17; 1 Cor. 14:23; 3 John 9; 1 Tim. 3:5; Acts 2:41–42; 2 Cor. 8:5; Acts 2:47; 1 Cor. 5:12–13; 1 Cor. 11:2; 2 Thess. 3:6; Rom. 16:17–20; 1 Cor. 11:23–24; Matt. 18:15–20; 1 Cor. 5:6; 2 Cor. 2:17; 1 Cor. 4:17; Matt. 28:20; John 14:15; John 15:12; 1 John 14:21; 1 Thess. 4:2; 2 John 6; Gal. 6:2;

Eph. 4:7; 1 Cor. 14:12; Phil. 1:1; Acts 14:23; Acts 15:22; 1 Tim. 3; Titus 1.

BFM2000
VI. The Church

A New Testament church of the Lord Jesus Christ is an autonomous local congregation of baptized believers, associated by covenant in the faith and fellowship of the gospel; observing the two ordinances of Christ, governed by His laws, exercising the gifts, rights, and privileges invested in them by His Word, and seeking to extend the gospel to the ends of the earth. **Each congregation operates under the Lordship of Christ through democratic processes.** In such a congregation each member is responsible and accountable to Christ as Lord. Its two scriptural offices are that of pastor/elder/overseer and deacon. While both men and women are gifted for service in the church, the office of pastor/elder/overseer is limited to men as qualified by Scripture.

The New Testament speaks also of the church as the Body of Christ which includes all of the redeemed of all the ages, believers from every tribe, and tongue, and people, and nation.

Matthew 16:15–19, 18:15–20; Acts 2:41–42,47, 5:11–14, 6:3–6, 13:1–3, 14:23,27, 15:1–30, 16:5, 20:28; Romans 1:7; 1 Corinthians 1:2, 3:16, 5:4–5, 7:17, 9:13–14, 12; Ephesians 1:22–23, 2:19–22, 3:8–11,21, 5:22–32; Philippians 1:1; Colossians 1:18; 1 Timothy 2:9–14, 3:1–15, 4:14; Hebrews 11:39–40; 1 Peter 5:1–4; Revelation 2–3, 21:2–3.

For space, I have only chosen to highlight two major confessions on each side of the Atlantic, but this concept is found in all the major Baptist confessions.

Contemporary Theological Implications

Recapturing a robust congregationalism will raise the bar as to how important it is to be a member of a local church. Sadly, in many churches it just doesn't mean all that much to be a member. Far too many churches take this Baptist distinctive very lightly. There's little difference in our churches between a member and a regular attender. Perhaps they can't vote at business or members meetings, but even that may not be that big of a loss if the church only has one or two meetings a year. Building this concept back up will help people see just how important their role is, and how important it will be when they will be "judging angels." We must recapture how important it is to possess the keys and be actively involved in admitting, releasing, and disciplining members. Again, this work is for the glory of God, the witness of the church, the health of the individual members, and — when necessary — the restoration of sinners. If we would raise the bar for what it means to be a member who holds the keys, it would certainly help the complementarian debates many are having. It would help us see the most important role in a church is not who can be pastor or elder, but who gets to be called "member"! This will help us to combat spurious arguments, such as those who say if you're a committed complementarian then you're "sidelining half your church from the Great Commission." That's simply not true. The Great Commission is the glorious privilege and responsibility of every member.

Practically

How can we recapture this distinctive? Particularly, here are ways to recapture the congregational aspect of who we are as Baptists.[10]

A simple way is to have regular members meetings where the church is equipped for this role. During these meetings, we should hear from and equip the congregation. We should hear updates and testimonies from church members. We should make space for updates on the church's missions' endeavors and local outreach. We should welcome in new members and release former members for other gospel tasks. If necessary, we should have a time where we handle cases of church discipline. Some of my sweetest memories from church are when men and women who were once on a path to destruction joyfully returned to the fold.

Finally, members meetings enable churches to remind the congregation and, if necessary, to vote on important documents of your church like bylaws, covenants, and statements of faith. This distinctive is a good reminder that God delights to use the weak things to shame the wise, and He certainly entrusts His work to jars of clay!

---

10 There is much more that could be said about being elder-led as well, but for the purposes of the book I focused primarily on what distinguishes us as Baptists. However, being elder-led has also been a part of our Baptist past. See Phil Newton's *Elders in the Life of the Church* and Mark Dever's *Polity*. In Dever's *Polity*, you will learn that the first ever Southern Baptist Convention President, W.B. Johnson, was a proponent of elder-led congregationalism.

Chapter 8

LIBERTY OF CONSCIENCE

A fourth Baptist distinctive is Liberty of Conscience.

This distinctive holds together the concepts of soul competency and religious liberty. As with the others, liberty of conscience also flows out of regenerate church membership. Because we Baptists prioritize the new birth for entrance into the New Covenant, we do not believe anyone can be born into the church. Instead, we are individually accountable before God (that's the concept of soul competency) nor can we be coerced into the church (that's the concept of religious liberty).

This Baptist distinctive connects to our ecclesiology. It shapes our understanding of the mission of the church. As mentioned above, soul competency means every person is individually accountable before God. For instance, neither your parents, nor your church, nor the state, can gain salvation for you. A text like Proverbs 9 highlights this: "For by me your days will be multiplied, and years will be added to your life. If you are wise, you are wise for yourself; if you scoff, you alone will bear it" (Prov. 9:11–12).

Soul competency is related to but not the same as the priesthood of all believers. The priesthood of all believers emerged out the Protestant Reformation. It stood over and against the expectation that believers needed priests as their mediator between them and the Lord. It affirms that all believers who are indwelt by the Spirit have access to God.

Unfortunately, over time, some thought that the priesthood of believers meant that we are all our own priest who can interpret Scripture however we want. I once heard a former liberal female professor from Southern Seminary explain to a Sunday School class how she concluded that she could be a pastor, "I wrestled with the Apostle Paul until he blessed me." It was her colloquial way of saying she got the interpretation she needed out of Paul.

But the priesthood of all believers doesn't mean we are now free to believe whatever we want, or that we can interpret the Scriptures however we want. Nor is interpretation solely an individual matter. Rather, to put it bluntly, it means we can approach God without a Roman Catholic priest. Soul competency is a soteriological matter that highlights our ability and our necessity to respond to God.

The other side of the liberty of conscience coin is religious liberty, which means that we all should be able to practice our faith without intrusion, interference, or coercion of civil governments. They have no sway over a person's conscience. B.H. Carroll, a Baptist from two generations ago, once wrote, "If one be responsible for himself, there must be no restraint or constraint of his conscience. Neither parent, nor government, nor church, may usurp the prerogative of God as Lord of the conscience. God himself does not coerce the will. His people are volunteers, not conscripts."[1] Baptists have expressed our belief in religious liberty dating back to at least

---

1 B.H. Carroll, *Baptists and Their Doctrines*. 18.

1614. Consider *Propositions and Conclusions Concerning True Christian Religion* which states:

> That the magistrate is not by virtue of his office to meddle with religion, or matters of conscience, to force and compel men to this or that form of religion or doctrine; but to leave Christian religion free, to every man's conscience, and to handle only civil transgressions (Rom. xiii), injuries and wrongs of man against man, in murder, adultery, theft, etc., for Christ only is the king, and lawgiver of the church and conscience (James iv. 12).

Later in the book, we'll look at a case study that pertains to liberty of conscience. But for now, it's important to see how this distinctive has been dear to us and flows out of our beliefs about conversion. Our forebears led the way on this precisely because they had been persecuted.

Their work on this topic caught the eye of profound political thinkers. In fact, when Lord Chancellor King in the 17th century tried to give credit to John Locke as the author of religious liberty, Locke replied, "The Baptists were the first and only propounders of absolute liberty — just and true liberty, equal and impartial liberty."[2]

This is because of what the above-quoted *Propositions and Conclusions* alludes to from James 4:12 on both soul competency and religious liberty, "There is only one lawgiver and judge, he who is able to save and to destroy. But who are you to judge your neighbor?"

We also need to take more time to consider 1 Corinthians. What does that book say about who the church has authority over? Paul is very clear: the church has no authority over the matters of the world or state, but only over the church and her members.

---

2 John Locke, *A Letter Concerning Toleration.*

Paul writes, "For what have I to do with judging outsiders? Is it not those inside the church whom you are to judge? God judges those outside. 'Purge the evil person from among you'" (1 Cor. 5:12–13). The church is not called to govern the world. But this raises some misconceptions and implications about religious liberty that need to be addressed. We turn our attention there now.

Implications

First, separation of church and state does not mean "we stay out of the government's business, and they stay out of ours."

We're called to be salt and light. We're called to be good neighbors. We're elect exiles who live for the good of those around us — which doesn't just mean their spiritual good, but the good of the whole person. This means, particularly in a democracy like ours, that we should be active in voting because we get to help determine who will be handed the sword (Romans 13). So we should vote and act in a civilly-minded way based on biblical principles for the good of our neighbors and families.

Second, however, church-sanctioned government has always gone poorly.

In the history of Christianity, whenever the "Christian state" has been able to use the sword to uphold Christianity, the arrangement has not gone well. Worse than that, this kind of arrangement has always led to false converts. We must remember precisely why Christ is more concerned with the heart than with outward behavior. Consider this lengthy quote again from John MacArthur's debate with R.C. Sproul about baptism. It's a helpful place to turn when we consider how Baptists differed from others, particularly the magisterial reformers, who sought to wed Reformation ideals to the State through the practice of paedobaptism.

MacArthur writes:

I am convinced that unless you have a regenerate church, you have chaos. But with the absolute church system in the national sovereign church, which, of course, the Catholic Church had all that power and the Reformers wanted some power to counter Rome, and so while Luther started out with a good intention of freedom of the conscience and all of that, eventually they started imposing everything on people and they.… I think they forced back in the infant baptism thing to create the state church control that could allow them to have a power base to fight against not only each other, the Lutheran fought the Reformed, but the Roman states also. State Christendom in every form, Catholic, Protestant, Lutheran and Reformed, I think, misunderstands New Testament church doctrine. And it's sad to think that Luther abandoned his original lofty idealism where he contended a Christianity of freedom and renouncing force and living by the Word and the Spirit and backed up into a state church perspective. But Luther said this, and I think this is maybe the truest expression of his heart. "I say that God wants no compulsory service. I say it a hundred thousand times, God wants no compulsory service. No one can or ought to be compelled to believe for the soul of man is an eternal thing above all that is temporal. Therefore only by an eternal Word must it be governed and grasped for it is simply insulting to govern in God's presence with human law and long custom. Neither the Pope, nor a Bishop, nor any other man has the right to decree a single syllable concerning a Christian man apart from his consent. All that comes to pass otherwise comes to pass in the spirit of tyranny." Sadly he allowed, I think, what he hated to take place. There's no … there's no tragedy greater, I don't think, coming out of the Reformation than the fact that the true church got executed, got stamped out under the massive weight of the state church system. There is no doctrine of the remnant in the New Testament, no such teaching. And I believe with sad darkening of Reformation light was the secularizing of the church, they brought back the very thing that Constantine had brought in it, they tried to get rid of. Sadly, modern Protestant Europe is as dark as old Catholic Europe. A state church and biblical Christianity are and always will be completely opposed to each other. The true church is not of this world, does not incorporate the unconverted. Infant baptism served the state church well, but horribly confuses the true church.[3]

Baptists have rightfully feared the state church because of what it can do to the conscience and how it can confuse the Church. So often, state churches turned against our Baptist forebearers, even by other professing believers. Again, to quote Carroll, "Christ wants volunteers not conscripts."[4]

Now let's consider what our theologians and confessions have said.

History and Confessions

English Baptist Thomas Helwys wrote this about the liberty of conscience:

> *Let the King judge, is it not most equal that men should choose their religion themselves, seeing they only must stand themselves before the judgment seat of God to answer for themselves…* . [We] profess and teach that in all earthly things the king's power is to be submitted unto; and in heavenly or spiritual things, if the king or any in authority under him shall exercise their power against any they are not to resist by any

---

3 John MacArthur, *"The Case for Believer's Baptism: The Credo Baptist Position"* https://www.gty.org/library/articles/A360/case-for-believers-baptism-the-credo-baptist-position (accessed Dec. 21, 2023).

4 See earlier Timothy George article *"Believer's Baptism."*

way or means, although it were in their power, but rather to submit
their lives as Christ and his disciples did, and yet keep their consciences
to God.[5]

John Leland, an American Baptist, and ardent defender of liberty of conscience, wrote:

> I now call for an instance, where Jesus Christ, the author of his reli-
> gious, or the apostles, who were divinely inspired, ever gave order to,
> or intimated that the civil powers on earth, ought to force people to
> observe the rules and doctrine of the gospel. *Mahomet (Mohammed)*
> *called in the sue of the law and sword, to convert people to his religion;*
> *but Jesus did not — does not* ... so there are many things that Jesus and
> the apostles taught, that men ought to obey, which yet the civil law has
> no concern in.[6]

George Truett, the longtime pastor of FBC Dallas, shared
these words from the steps of the U.S. Capitol before the 1920
Southern Baptist Convention:

> Their contention now, is, and has been, and, please God, must ever be,
> that it is the natural and fundamental and indefeasible right of every
> human being to worship God or not, according to the dictates of his
> conscience, and, as long as he does not infringe upon the rights of oth-
> ers, he is to be held accountable alone to God for all religious beliefs
> and practices... God wants free worshippers and no other kind... Bap-
> tists regard as an enormity any attempt to force the conscience, or to

---

5 Thomas Helwys, *A Short Declaration of the Mystery of Iniquity*, ed. Richard Groves (Mercer
   University Press, 1998).
6 John Leland, *The Writings of John Leland*. 187.

constrain men, by outward penalties, to this or that form of religious belief.[7]

For the space of this book, I will limit the number of confessions, but there are many. As has already been pointed out, this goes back as far as 1614 in England. But here are some others to consider.

First London
XLVIII.

A civil magistracy is an ordinance of God, set up by Him for the punishment of evil doers, and for the praise of them that do well; and that in all lawful things, commanded by them, subjection ought to be given by us in the Lord, not only for wrath, but for conscience sake; and that we are to make supplications and prayers for kings, and all that are in authority, that under them we may live a quiet and peaceable life, in all godliness and honesty. Rom. 13:1,2, etc.; 1 Pet. 2:13,14; 1 Tim. 2:1,2,3. **Note:** The supreme magistracy of this kingdom we acknowledge to be the king and parliament (now established) freely chosen by the kingdom, and that we are to maintain and defend all civil laws and civil officers made by them, which are for the good of the commonwealth. And we acknowledge with thankfulness, that God hath made this present king and parliament honorable in throwing down the prelatical hierarchy, because of their tyranny and oppression over us, under which this kingdom long groaned, for which we are ever engaged to bless God, and honor them for the same. And concerning the worship of God; there is but one lawgiver, which is able to save and destroy, James 4:12; which is Jesus Christ, who hath given laws and rules sufficient in His word

---

7 George Truett, "*Baptists and Religious Liberty*" address at 1920 Southern Baptist Convention: https://bjconline.org/wp-content/uploads/2014/03/Baptists-and-Religious-Liberty.pdf, accessed Dec. 19, 2023).

for His worship; and for any to make more, were to charge Christ with want of wisdom, or faithfulness, or both, in not making laws enough, or not good enough for His house: Surely it is our wisdom, duty, and privilege, to observe Christ's laws only, Ps 2:6,9,10,12. So it is the magistrates duty to tender the liberty of mens' consciences, Eccles. 8:8 (which is the tenderest thing unto all conscientious men, and most dear unto them, and without which all other liberties will not be worth the naming, much less enjoying) and to protect all under them from all wrong, injury, oppression and molestation; so it is our duty not to be wanting in nothing which is for their honor and comfort, and whatsoever is for the wellbeing of the commonwealth wherein we live; it is our duty to do, and we believe it to be our express duty, especially in matters of religion, to be fully persuaded in our minds of the lawfulness of what we do, as knowing whatsoever is not of faith is sin. And as we cannot do anything contrary to our understandings and consciences, so neither can we forebear the doing of that which our understandings and consciences bind us to do. And if the magistrate should require us to do otherwise, we are to yield our persons in a passive way to their power, as the saints of old have done, James 5:4. And thrice happy shall he be, that shall lose his life for witnessing (though but for the least tittle) of the truth of the Lord Jesus Christ, 1 Pet. 5; Gal. 5.

New Hampshire Confession
XVI.
Of the Civil Government

We believe that civil government is of divine appointment, for the interests and good order of human society; and that magistrates are to be prayed for, conscientiously honored, and obeyed; except only in things opposed to the will of our Lord Jesus Christ, who is the only Lord of the conscience, and the Prince of the kings of the earth. Rom. 13:1–7; Deu. 16:18; 2 Sam. 23:3; Ex. 18:23; Jer. 30:21; Matt. 22:21; Titus 3:1; 1 Peter 2:13; 1 Tim. 2:1–4; Acts 5:29; Matt. 28; Dan. 3:15–18; Dan. 6:7-10; Acts 4:18–20; Matt. 23:10; Rom. 14:4; Rev. 19:16; Ps. 72:11; Ps. 2; Rom. 14:9–13.

BFM2000
XVII. Religious Liberty

God alone is Lord of the conscience, and He has left it free from the doctrines and commandments of men which are contrary to His Word or not contained in it. Church and state should be separate. The state owes to every church protection and full freedom in the pursuit of its spiritual ends. In providing for such freedom no ecclesiastical group or denomination should be favored by the state more than others. Civil government being ordained of God, it is the duty of Christians to render loyal obedience thereto in all things not contrary to the revealed will of God. The church should not resort to the civil power to carry on its work. The gospel of Christ contemplates spiritual means alone for the pursuit of its ends. The state has no right to impose penalties for religious opinions of any kind. The state has no right to impose taxes for the support of any form of religion. A free church in a free state is the Christian ideal, and this implies the right of free and unhindered access to God on the part of all men, and the right to form and propagate opinions in the sphere of religion without interference by the civil power.

Genesis 1:27; 2:7; Matthew 6:6–7,24, 16:26, 22:21; John 8:36; Acts 4:19–20; Romans 6:1–2, 13:1–7; Galatians 5:1,13; Philippians 3:20; 1 Timothy 2:1–2; James 4:12; 1 Peter 2:12–17, 3:11–17, 4:12–19.

Conclusion

We'll think more about the practical effects of this particular distinctive later in the book with a chapter devoted to a current case study that touches on this Baptist conviction.

Chapter 9

BAPTIST DISTINCTIVES
CONCLUSION

We partner together according to these distinctives because we believe we have something to give the world. Yes, we primarily want to give the world the gospel. But that's not all. We believe our ecclesiological commitments undergird our gospel proclamation. They accompany the gospel wherever it goes. Dagg put it like this a century ago:

> Church order and the ceremonials of religion, are less important than a new heart; and in the view of some, any laborious investigation of questions respecting them may appear to be needless and unprofitable. But we know, from the Holy Scriptures, that Christ gave commands on these subjects, and we cannot refuse to obey. Love prompts our obedience; and love prompts also the search which may be necessary to ascertain his will. Let us, therefore, prosecute the investigations which are before us, with a fervent prayer, that the Holy Spirit, who guides

into all truth, may assist us to learn the will of him whom we supremely love and adore.[1]

The regeneration of unbelievers is our paramount concern, but that doesn't mean we're unconcerned with our ecclesiological convictions. As stated earlier in the book, we are doctrinally aligned for an evangelistic purpose. The Scriptures are clear: the church is the foundation of the truth we are to share with the world (1 Timothy 3:15). For these reasons, even as we're committed to local church autonomy, Baptists cooperate in global missions. Even in our independence, we are interdependent for the cause of Christ in the world.[2]

Our commitment to this sort of cooperation has driven Baptist cooperative efforts on both sides of the Pond. It drove the formation of the Association of Irish Baptist Churches. In 1895, twenty-seven Irish Baptist churches formalized themselves into an association after breaking from the Baptist Union amidst the Downgrade Controversy.[3] Now, more than 125 years later, that Association has grown by over 100 churches. It still exists to share resources and establish new works.

Baptist cooperation in America has cooperative missions to thank for its formation. The great Baptist missionary Adoniram Judson set off to the East as a congregationalist. And yet, after searching the Scriptures in order to refute William Carey's credobaptist convictions, Judson became a convinced credobaptist himself. This led to Luther Rice, his fellow missionary, to return home and sever ties

---

1 J. L. Dagg, *Manual of Church Order* (Charleston, SC: Southern Baptist Publication Society, 1858), 12.

2 I have written more about this in an article entitled "Partnering Together to Plant" 9 Marks Journal, Church Planting. https://www.9marks.org/article/partnering-together-to-plant/

3 See the story of the Association of Baptist Churches in Ireland: https://www.baptistsinireland.org/about/our-story/ (accessed, Mar. 15, 2024).

with their supporting Congregationalist churches. Rice also had to raise support from Baptist congregations in America. All this led to the formation of the *General Missionary Convention of the Baptist Denomination in the United States of America for Foreign Missions* in 1814. This convention became known as the "Triennial" convention because it met every three years. In 1845, this convention split over issues related to slavery, which led to the formation of the SBC.[4]

Several years ago, I wrestled with these distinctives and wondered if I could be committed to their propagation. Eventually, I realized that I loved these distinctives. I believed they represented sound New Testament ecclesiology and missiology. I'm a convinced Baptist, and because I am, I love this response from Spurgeon to his mother — one that I hope will be believed and felt by all my fellow committed Baptists. Upon learning he had become a Baptist, she was upset. Here's what she wrote, "Ah, Charles, I often prayed the Lord to make you a Christian, but I never asked that you might become a Baptist." Spurgeon wrote back with his normal wit, "Ah, Mother, the Lord had answered your prayer with His usual bounty, and has given you exceeding abundantly above what you asked or thought."[5]

---

4 For more information on the Triennial Convention and the formation of the SBC, check out chapters 5 and 6 of Chute, Finn, and Haykin's *The Baptist Story: From English Sect to Global Movement*. Broadman and Holman Publishing: Nashville. 115-162.

5 Spurgeon. *Autobiography*. 68.

PART 2

HOW WE CAN HOLD THESE
CONVICTIONS WELL

Chapter 10

COURAGEOUSLY AND COMPASSIONATELY

(1 Corinthians 16:13b–14)

It's important to consider how to hold our convictions well. We must be courageous and compassionate, especially in our current context. To quote my dad again, "What you say is most important but how you say it has never been more important." Paul gets to this concept in 1 Corinthians 16:13–14 when he wrote, "Act like men and be strong."

We should hold to our confessions and convictions courageously. The phrase "act like men" is one word in the Greek. It could literally be translated "be manly." The next command — "be strong" — is for men and women. The apostle seems to be singling out men because women are usually more steadfast in the faith. But also because men, especially young men, need to be told to grow up and live with mettle, to have guts. This military language calls for men to be courageous, not cowardly. The Septuagint — the Greek translation of the Old Testament — uses the phrase during the conquest of the land. It's a call to act confidently in the promises of God who upholds all things by the word of His power.

It's a reminder to be men of valor who do not waiver in the face of a fallen world.

The phrase "act like men" calls to mind an infamous scene from the reign of Bloody Mary. She executed 288 English Protestants for their faith. Two of them were Hugh Latimer and Nicholas Ridley. When they were about to be burnt at the stake, Latimer famously turned to his friend Ridley and said, "Be of good cheer, Ridley, and play the man. We shall this day by God's grace, light up such a candle in England, as I trust will never be put out."[6] Latimer was right. They did indeed light a fire, the embers of which we are the beneficiaries of even to this day! It's very unlikely we'll ever have to pay the same price for our convictions as Latimer and Ridley. But whatever we face, may we have the same kind of confidence.

But we also should hold to these things compassionately. Paige Patterson, perhaps ironically to some, warns of this passage:

> Unfortunately, efforts to accomplish the commands of V. 13 frequently precipitate behavior patterns that are less than charitable. Therefore, Paul reminded the Corinthians that it was essential that even the Christian's warfare be motivated by godliness. One might be watchful, stand fast in the faith, approach the conflict like men, and pursue the enemy, and do it all without love. The whole point of 1 Corinthians 13 is to warn against the impropriety of the exercise of spiritual virtues in the absence of love.[7]

---

6 Foxe's *Book of Martyrs*. CHAPTER XVI, Persecutions in England During the Reign of Queen Mary.

7 Patterson, Paige. *The Troubled Triumphant Church*. 317.

So, Paul says, "*Let all that you do be done in love.*"

Love is a dominant theme throughout 1 Corinthians, especially chapter 13. That's instructive in a book that features so much rebuke. Paul even ends the book by reminding them of his own affection for them, "My love is with you all" (1 Corinthians 16:24). In doing so, Paul is an example of how to hold on to our convictions courageously and compassionately. He didn't shrink from declaring to them what they needed to hear, but he does so as a teacher who loves them. Schreiner says, "The exhortation to toughness must never be interpreted as squelching tenderness and affection, nor should love be interpreted as mere sentimentality or softness."[8]

My favorite memory verse growing up was "Jesus wept." You know why! It was easy to memorize and thus get a prize. But as I've gotten older, that verse has taken on so much more significance. It speaks to the man of sorrows who is acquainted with grief. We should be tough and tender just like our Lord who stood down the religious leaders and stood weeping over the city of Jerusalem that would crucify Him.

Elsewhere, Paul tells us that we must speak the truth in love (Ephesians 4:15). As those who have the truth and as those who have been reborn in love, we must hold these two together. John Piper once wrote, "Truth aims at love and love aims at truth.... For love shapes *how* to speak the truth while truth shapes *how* to show love."[9] On matters of first importance, we will not back down or falter. In matters of secondary importance that touch on our ecclesiological convictions, we will be resolute because we believe the church is God's chosen means to accomplish His purposes in the world. We

---

8 Schreiner, Thomas. 1 Corinthians, TNTC. 333.
9 John Piper, "*Truth and Love*" https://www.desiringgod.org/articles/truth-and-love (accessed Dec. 19, 2023).

should have Paul's posture in Galatians 2:5, "To them we did not yield in submission even for a moment, so that the truth of the gospel might be preserved for you." We must be concerned if people are swerving from the truth, but at the same time, the aim of our charge is love (1 Timothy 1:5). We do not want to be squishy like the progressive left, nor shrill like the hyper-fundamentalist right.

We stand strong and contend for the Faith. But we do so with winsome, seasoned, gracious speech. There's a middle ground between calling names and disagreeing with humility. We will explore this more in our case studies to come, but on issues that are clear in our confessions — inerrancy, penal substitution, the deity of Christ, salvation by grace through faith, believer's baptism by immersion, regenerate church membership, complementarianism, etc. — there is no third way or middle ground. On clear ethical issues like abortion, homosexuality, transgenderism, etc., there is no third way or middle ground. Yet that is part of the issue, people can agree on these issues and if they are not as adamant on abolition or as vocal and energized politically on social media, then they are labeled liberal compromisers, even if they hold to the first- and second-tier issues of theological agreement. There's much to consider here about how we interact with fellow Christians when we disagree.

Those gripped by the gospel and our Baptist distinctives should be different. Just consider Ephesians 4:

> I therefore, a prisoner for the Lord, urge you to walk in a manner worthy of the calling to which you have been called, with all **humility and gentleness, with patience, bearing with one another in love, eager to maintain the unity of the Spirit in the bond of peace**.... And he gave the apostles, the prophets, the evangelists, the shepherds and teachers, to equip the saints for the work of ministry, for building up the body of Christ, until we all attain to the unity of the faith and of the knowledge

of the Son of God, **to mature manhood**, to the measure of the stature of the fullness of Christ, so that we may no longer be children, tossed to and fro by the waves and carried about by every wind of doctrine, by human cunning, by craftiness in deceitful schemes. **Rather, speaking the truth in love, we are to grow up** in every way into him who is the head, into Christ, [16] from whom the whole body, joined and held together by every joint with which it is equipped, when each part is working properly, makes the body grow so that it builds itself up in love (Eph. 4:1–3, 11–16).

Those attracted to the progressive left need to be reminded that you can't "speak the truth in love" if you're not speaking the truth at all. There's no such thing as a loving lie. Those attracted to the hyper-fundamentalist right need to be reminded how important it is to maintain a posture of grace and love. They need to remember their aim is building others up, not their tearing them down. As Paul reminds us, "Let no corrupting talk come out of your mouths, but only such as is good for building up, as fits the occasion, that it may give grace to those who hear" (Ephesians 4:29).

It's a sad day when people say, "We should be about the truth" and someone says, "Yeah, but." But it's also a sad day when people say, "We must be loving" and someone else says, "Yeah, but." It's a sad day when sticking to a clearly defined confession of faith is dismissed by some, as "fundamentalism"; at the same time, it's a sad day when "winsome" is seen as a swear word.

Again, on first-tier issues that mark us out as Christians and second-tier ecclesiological issues that mark us out as Baptists, we will stand our ground. But we must remember: not every issue is so clear. Not every issue requires us to nail 95 Theses to a Wittenberg door.

With that in mind, let's turn to two case studies to try to make the point.

Chapter 11

CASE STUDY: CHRISTIAN NATIONALISM

As a convictional, confessional, courageous, and compassionate Baptist, I would like to consider an example that touches on a Baptist distinctive — liberty of conscience — and our Baptist confessions. The issue is theonomy and Christian Nationalism.[1]

---

1 Definitions for the terms "Christian Nationalism" and "theonomy" may be harder to give in our day given the rise in such arguments and the nuances that come with critique, and I seek to give a more popular level definition of Christian Nationalism later in this chapter. However, some basic definitions might serve the purpose of this chapter. Theonomy is the belief that modern societies should be governed by divine law, primarily including the judicial laws of the Old Testament, though certain theonomists might nuance exactly which laws and how to apply them. Consider Andrew Walker's helpful description of current Christian Nationalism: "Government has a duty to promote true religion. Christianity is true religion. Therefore, government has a duty to promote Christianity..." thus, "... The church looks to the state to suppress heresy; Christianity is given official favor by the state; Church and state are formally united; *The state takes active interest in cultivating and protecting Christian doctrine; Religious toleration is extended only so far as the religion in question does not disturb sound order; Non-Christians are subject to a form of second-class dhimmitude; Heretics and non-believers could potentially be executed*" (emphasis is mine). Walker's definition can be accessed: https://www.9marks.org/article/a-baptist-engagement-with-the-case-for-christian-nationalism/.

I hope this exercise will help us see why confessions are helpful guides in interpretation. I also hope we'll see how important it is to hold strongly to our convictions in a compassionate and cheerful way. I share many concerns that overlap with those who identify as Christian Nationalists. I'm particularly concerned with the decay of common-grace, largely Judeo-Christian values. I'm horrified by the complete dismissal of God's created order regarding gender and sexuality. I love living in America. I love the freedoms we enjoy. By and large, I'm thankful we've been able to live in a 1 Timothy 2 society where we can live a "peaceful and quiet life, godly and dignified in every way" (1 Tim. 2:2b).

In a democracy, there's a sense in which voters hand the sword to someone. So as voters we shouldn't forget that we're Christians. We should be concerned about how our leaders will or will not uphold Christian values, how they will or will not encourage violations of natural law when it comes to their positions on abortion, sexuality, and gender.

I do think the tendency among some evangelicals to "hug left and punch right" is strange. One group expresses outrage at Donald Trump showing up at Robert Jeffress' church, but they don't say a thing about the mayor of Chicago being honored at Charlie Dates' church. I agree we should be civically active and vote in line with Christian principles. And yet, I have concerns about Christian Nationalism in line with what I have been trying to say throughout this book.

For some, the argument goes something like this, "You will have an authoritarianism and nationalism of some kind so it will either be secular religion or Christian religion." But our approach to this topic isn't always so nice and tidy. We have already explored our Baptist distinctives and why Baptists historically would have had issue with this form of Christian Nationalism. And yet, my concern in keeping with the argument of this book falls into the categories of emphasis, tone, and Scriptural warrant.

Emphasis

The concern about misplaced emphasis hit home to me years ago. Several years back, I had a Christian friend who worked in politics. The moment Obamacare was passed, she posted 51 tweets in 60 minutes blasting that decision. Now you can have opinions about that legislation, and I certainly have my own. But what struck me as I read her tweets was that in the five years I had known her and followed her on social media, I had never seen her post 51 things about Jesus, His church, or His commission. We all have things we get energized about, but I can't help but think what matters most to us comes out in what we say. Or we might say, "Out of the abundance of the heart the fingers tweet … or X … or whatever we call it now!" What energizes us most? Issues clearly connected to the mission of the church or issues more intimately connected to the things of this earth?

Tone

I've seen influential people who identify as Christian Nationalists who are more than happy to call those with whom they disagree "bozos," "dopes," or "losers." This is a danger for any group that becomes super convictional. In our zeal, we dismiss, label, and belittle others. May it not be so among us.

Scriptural Warrant

Ironically, some are using the Great Commission as Scriptural warrant for this new form of Christian Nationalism. They say something akin to "we are called to disciple the nations," and by that they mean the nation-states, not the *ethne* (meaning "the peoples"). However, if that is the case, then that's the only place in the New Testament that gives such a directive. Nowhere in the New Testament are we told to "Christianize the government." Nowhere are we told that's part of the mission of the church. Nowhere in Acts are the disciples hatching plans to infiltrate the Sanhedrin and reinstitute a Christian-influenced theocracy. Nowhere in Romans does Paul give instructions on how to oust Nero and Christianize the Roman Republic (instead, Peter exhorts us to "honor the emperor," 1 Pet. 2:17). Nowhere in 1 Corinthians does he give instructions for how to do this in Corinth. Nowhere are we told to reinstitute blasphemy laws. Rather, Paul says, "Is it not those inside the church we are to judge? God judges those on the outside" (1 Corinthians 5:12–13).

As I have been talking to my international brothers about Christian Nationalism, I realize this is uniquely an American issue. That gets to the point: Christ's kingdom is not of this world.

Why Bring This Up At All?

This gets at the heart of why being convictional combined with being confessional matters. Certainly, there are times we need to add material to our confessions. For example, many Baptists have added articles on matters of sexuality and gender in our current day. But if the newest issue of debate and consideration is specific to a certain context and not obvious to brothers or sisters who live elsewhere, then it probably shouldn't make a dent in our historic confessions. These confessions aren't inerrant, but they do direct our attention to the truths most clearly articulated in the Scriptures, truths that have endured for centuries and throughout countless contexts, which guide us through the debates of today.

Chapter 12

CASE STUDY: COMPLEMENTARIANISM AND THE OFFICE OF PASTOR

Another case study to consider as we think about being confessional, convictional, and courageous is complementarianism. A presenting example is the conversation around whether "pastoring" is a gift or an office.[2] Recently, men like Sam Storms, Eric Geiger, Jason Parades, and Rick Warren have argued that the term "pastor" (ποιμήν) is not referring to an office but a gift. Therefore, the "pastor" of Ephesians 4:11 is not synonymous with the office of elder/overseer from 1 Timothy 3. Further back, Harold Hoehner made this same argument with more detailed exegesis. This argument, however, does not

---

2 This is a summary of a larger paper I did on this topic for a PhD Class on Pastoral Theology, Southeastern Baptist Theological Seminary, August 2023.

stand up biblically, nor does it stand the test of time and confessions that guide proper interpretation.[3]

To give them a fair hearing, here are the basics of their argument. Storms argues that pastoring is simply a gift. Though many elders will have the gift of pastoring, some non-elders will have the gift of pastoring. Storms writes,

> The only texts where the verb to shepherd or to pastor is used of leaders in the local church are Acts 20:28 and 1 Peter 5:2. In the former Paul is addressing the Elders at Ephesus, and in the latter Peter is likewise giving instructions to Elders.... Clearly, these two texts where the verb is used indicate that an essential role or ministry of the Elders in a local church is to shepherd or to pastor the people of God. Thus, it stands to reason that all Elders must, in some sense, be pastors. But nothing in the way this verb is used should lead us to believe that all pastors must be Elders. No text asserts the latter.... There is *only one text* where the noun "shepherd" or "pastor" is used of leaders in the local church (Eph. 4:11). In this latter text, Paul is identifying several representative gifts that Christ has given to the church. We know that prophets are those with the gift of prophecy and that evangelists are those with the gift of evangelism and that teachers are those with the gift of teaching. Whether or not apostleship is a spiritual gift or office (in some sense of

---

3 I put this in the category of complementarianism because although most of the men identified in this chapter would consider themselves complementarians, it is not in keeping with a historic complementarianism that views the role of pastor as synonymous with that of the office of elder and as only to be filled by qualified men, and as we will see in this chapter, nor is it with our confessions. Mary Kassian helpfully defines complementarianism and egalitarianism when she writes, "the label 'complementarian' has only been in use for about 25 years. It was coined by a group of scholars who got together to try and come up with a word to describe someone who ascribes to the historic, biblical idea that male and female are equal, but different. The need for such a label arose in response to the proposition that equality means role-interchangeability (egalitarianism) — a concept first forwarded and popularized in evangelical circles in the 1970s and 1980s by 'Biblical Feminists'" (Mary Kassian, "Complementarianism for Dummies," Sep. 4, 2012. Accessed at: https://www.thegospelcoalition.org/article/complementarianism-for-dummies/)

the term) is a debatable question. It would seem, then, that we should conclude that pastors are those with the gift of pastoring. Contrary to what many in the charismatic world believe, there is nothing in this text that would lead us to conclude that Paul is identifying five specific offices or governmental positions.... . These five nouns refer to people who were blessed with a particular gift, not a position of authority in the local church. Of course, apostles are of a different order and did exercise authority over churches.[4]

Hoehner argues similarly: "Scripture consistently maintains a distinction between the office and the gift. Eldership is an office, whereas pastor-teacher is a gift."[5] Hoehner essentially argues that gifts are given to every Christian, while offices are not; therefore, the list in Ephesians 4:11 has to do with gifts (potentially) given to every Christian. Consistent with Hoehner, some might argue that all Christians are called to care for others. So, in one sense, all Christians "pastor." Hoehner makes a similar argument — one that will be seen as inconsistent with the usage of the term "pastor" in the New Testament — when he writes, "On the other hand, it may be that Paul was encouraging elders to care for believers in Ephesus in the more general way that all Christians are to care for one another rather than their having that specific gift."[6]

First and foremost, it's important to examine whether this position withstands the scrutiny of Scriptures, because the Scriptures alone are inerrant. Then we must consider this position alongside our confessions as guides to our interpretation. Then we can ask if

---

4 Storms, "Is it Biblically Permissible for a Woman to be Called a 'Pastor'?": https:// samstorms.org/enjoying-god-blog/post/is-it-biblically-permissible-for-a-woman-to-be-called-a -pastor (accessed Aug. 3, 2023).

5 Hoehner, "Can a Woman Be a Pastor-Teacher?" JETS Journal, Dec. 2007, 763.

6 Hoehner, "Can a Woman Be a Pastor-Teacher?" 766.

the confessions (and thus church history) are consistent with a position like the one espoused by Hoehner and Storms. Simply put, this position does not stand up under that examination.

The dominant position of church history has recognized pastor as a synonymous term with the office of elder/overseer. This is a good example of how confessions help us move away from novel interpretations of the text.

Biblically

The Greek word for "office" (ἐπισκοπή) is only used four times in the New Testament and only translated as "office" twice (Acts 1:20; 1 Tim 3:1). In Acts 1:20, it is used for the office of "apostle." In 1 Timothy 3:1, it represents the office of "overseer," which is followed by a list of qualifications for the office which mirrors the qualifications for "elders" in Titus 1. Importantly, this connection reveals that at least one of the gifts mentioned in Ephesians 4:11, apostle is also an office. It's consistent therefore for the other specific office mentioned as an office to show up in the Ephesians 4 list, that of overseer or elder.

Use of "Pastor"

The term "pastor" as a noun (ποιμήν) occurs eighteen times in the New Testament — six times of actual shepherds, eleven times of the Chief Shepherd, and once of spiritual shepherds (Ephesians 4:11). In 1 Peter 2:25, Jesus is called both the "Shepherd [Pastor] and Overseer [Bishop] of our souls." Peter is pleased to connect the terms "pastor" and "overseer" in strengthening his explanation of who Jesus is for His flock.

Use of "To Pastor"

The strongest argument for seeing pastor and elder/overseer as synonymous terms is the use of the verb form of *pastor* in the New Testament. The term "to pastor" (ποιμαίνω) is used eleven times in the New Testament — three times of actual shepherds, three times of elders (spiritual shepherds), and five times of Jesus as the Chief Shepherd. Interestingly, outside of physical shepherds and the Chief Shepherd, the charge "to pastor" is only given to elders (John 21:16; Acts 20:28; 1 Peter 5:2). It's never given to every Christian as though all could possess it as a gift. In addition, the three words for "pastor," "elder," and "overseer" all show up together in some form twice in the New Testament. In both instances, elders are being addressed and told "to pastor" the flock or church of God (Acts 20:28; 1 Peter 5:2).

Again, this charge "to pastor" is only given to actual shepherds, the Chief Shepherd, and elders, not any or every Christian. If "to pastor" only refers to a gifting given to any Christian, Ephesians 4:11 would be the only place in the New Testament where that was so. The burden of proof, then, lies with those who would argue it is simply a gift, considering that this charge "to pastor" is only given to elders as pertains to the church.

But what do our historic confessions say?

Confessions

Proper interpretation must be informed by how the church has interpreted a text throughout history. Our confessions reveal the fruit of this labor. It will be demonstrated that across the centuries and traditions (not just Baptist Confessions and theologians) the term "pastor" has been viewed synonymously with the office of elder. Men like Chrysostom, Gregory the Great, Martin Bucer, John Calvin, and Richard Baxter — to name a few — have viewed the term "pastor" as synonymous with the office of elder/overseer. In fact, Calvin says this plainly in the *Institutes of the Christian Religion,* "In giving the name of bishops, presbyters, and pastors, indiscriminately to those who govern churches, I have done it on the authority of Scripture, which uses the words as synonymous."[7]

Now to the confessions. Interestingly, across several different traditions (Reformed, Presbyterian, Anglican, and in our own Baptist heritage) the confessions view pastor as an office and not *only* a gift. We do not just find this in the *BFM2000,* but many others. In fact, I have been unable to find a confession that makes the same argument as Hoehner, Storms, Geiger, Parades, and Warren.[8]

Augsburg Confession (1531)

It was also said that one could obtain more merit through the monastic life than through all other walks of life, which had been ordered by God, such as the office of pastor or preacher, the office of ruler, prince, lord, and the like.[9]

Book of Common Prayer (1789)

In the American Anglican tradition, the *Book of Common Prayer* equates the office of bishop and pastor. *The Book of Common Prayer* has prayers for pastors that states,

> N (name of Bishop)., Bishop in the Church of God, the clergy and people of the Diocese of N., trusting in the guidance of the Holy Spirit, have chosen N.N. to be a bishop and chief pastor. We therefore ask you

---

7 John Calvin, *Institutes of Christian Religion,* Pantianos Classics (London: Reinolde Wolf & Richarde Harisson, 1539; Reprint and translation to English, 1581), 376.

8 The only significant traditions that did not have a confession demonstrating that pastor is an office and not just a gift were Assemblies of God and Methodists, and neither mentioned offices at all nor made the argument that pastor was only a gift.

9 The Augsburg Confession can be found online at https://www.faithdc.org/uploads/1/4/3/0/14306368/the_augsburg_confession.pdf

to lay your hands upon him and in the power of the Holy Spirit to consecrate him a bishop in the one, holy, catholic, and apostolic Church.[1]

In addition, the *Book of Common Prayer* never identifies pastor as a gift, but rather places pastor alongside the office of bishop when it states,

O God, our heavenly Father, who raised up your faithful servant N., to be a [bishop and] pastor in your Church and to feed your flock: Give abundantly to all pastors the gifts of your Holy Spirit, that they may minister in your household as true servants of Christ and stewards of your divine mysteries; through Jesus Christ our Lord, who lives and reigns with you and the Holy Spirit, one God, for ever and ever. Amen.[2]

Westminster Larger Catechism (1647)

The Presbyterian Westminster Larger Catechism states in chapter 30,

The Lord Jesus, as King and Head of his church, hath therein appointed a government, in the hand of church officers, distinct from the civil magistrate.[3]

In the footnotes of this chapter pertaining to church officers, the WLC quotes Acts 20:17, 28 and 1 Timothy 5:17, which both mention elders before quoting Ephesians 4:11.[4]

---

1 The Episcopal Church, *The Book of Common Prayer* (New York: Church Publishing, 2007), 513, https://www.episcopalchurch.org/wp-content/uploads/sites/2/2023/06/book_of_common_prayer.pdf - please note the parenthesis with N is a formula to be used for the name of the Bishop being put forward.

2 The Episcopal Church, *The Book of Common Prayer*, 248.

3 Westminster Confession, 142, https://www.pcaac.org/wp-content/uploads/2022/04/WCFScripureProofs2022.pdf

4 Westminster Confession, 143.

Baptist Faith and Message 1963 and 2000

In the Baptist tradition, both the *Baptist Faith and Message 1963 and 2000* call pastor an office, interestingly doing so in the same article as the *Baptist Faith and Message 1925*, which uses the term "elders" rather than "pastors."[5] The word usage clearly shows that this office is one and the same.

BFM1963

VI. THE CHURCH

A New Testament church of the Lord Jesus Christ is a local body of baptized believers who are associated by covenant in the faith and fellowship of the gospel, observing the two ordinances of Christ, committed to His teachings, exercising the gifts, rights, and privileges invested in them by His Word, and seeking to extend the gospel to the ends of the earth. This church is an autonomous body, operating through democratic processes under the Lordship of Jesus Christ. In such a congregation members are equally responsible. Its Scriptural officers are pastors and deacons. The New Testament speaks also of the church as the body of Christ which includes all of the redeemed of all the ages.

BFM2000

VI. The Church

A New Testament church of the Lord Jesus Christ is an autonomous local congregation of baptized believers, associated by covenant in the faith and fellowship of the gospel; observing the two ordinances of Christ, governed by His laws, exercising the gifts, rights, and privileges invested in them by His Word, and seeking to

---

5 This was made even more clear with the addition of "elder/overseer" to the BFM2000 at the 2023 Southern Baptist Convention in New Orleans.

extend the gospel to the ends of the earth. Each congregation operates under the Lordship of Christ through democratic processes. In such a congregation each member is responsible and accountable to Christ as Lord. Its two scriptural offices are that of pastor/elder/overseer and deacon. While both men and women are gifted for service in the church, the office of pastor/elder/overseer is limited to men as qualified by Scripture.

The New Testament speaks also of the church as the Body of Christ which includes all of the redeemed of all the ages, believers from every tribe, and tongue, and people, and nation.

Second London Baptist Confession (1689)

Further back the Second London Confession also makes this clear connection when it reads,

Although it be incumbent on the bishops or pastors of the churches, to be instant in preaching the word, by way of office, yet the work of preaching the word is not so peculiarly confined to them but that others also gifted and fitted by the Holy Spirit for it, and approved and called by the church, may and ought to perform it (Acts 11:19–21; 1 Peter 4:10, 11).[6]

Conclusion

There certainly might be resources on this topic that may not have been found. But it appears that this argument *didn't show up until*

---

6 Second London Confession, Chapter 26, Article 11, p. 26. -https://www.grbc.net/wp-content/uploads/2015/09/The-1689-Baptist-Confession-of-Faith.pdf. It is important to note that in neither the Methodist tradition nor the Assemblies of God do they make any statement about offices in the Church. However, neither do they try to propose that the term "pastor" is a gift and not an office. It is interesting that even a cursory look at churches in both traditions will find pastors as the main leaders of the church, at least implying that the term "pastor" is also used for the office among their traditions.

2002. Interestingly, even Hoehner did not make this argument in his 1985 commentary. In fact, he made an argument in that work very similar to what the majority of church history makes.[7] It raises the question, why the change? The change of culture on issues of gender must be considered. Nonetheless, novel interpretations of Holy Scripture should be viewed with great skepticism. That's why confessions continue to be so helpful. They provide doctrinal moorings through any storm.

This demonstrates another reason we need to be confessional and courageous as issues arise. If some issue has not shown up in any confession, it does not necessarily make it wrong. But it should raise some serious questions about its validity. That's why confessions are vital to both biblical fidelity and missional cooperation. Indeed, in this regard, confessionalism remains a most important issue for us as Baptists. We believe the local church is the headquarters of our mission. So it stands to reason that whoever leads those *local* headquarters is of paramount importance.

---

7   Hoehner in his 1985 commentary makes a connection between the pastor-teacher of Eph 4:11 with the overseer of 1 Timothy 3 and the elder of Titus 1 when he writes, "They refer to two characteristics of the same person who is pastoring believers (by comforting and guiding) while at the same time instructing them in God's ways (overseers or elders are to be able to teach; 1 Tim. 3:2; Titus 1:9)." Hoehner, "Ephesians," in *The Bible Knowledge Commentary: An Exposition of the Scriptures*, Victor Books, 635.

Chapter 13

CONCLUSION: FORGIVEN CORINTHIANS

I'm unsure what the future holds for us Baptists, but like our past, it needs to be more confessional, convictional, courageous, compassionate, and cheerful. E. Y. Mullins preached a sermon at the 1923 SBC entitled, "The Dangers and Duties of this Present Hour." What he said continues to the present time. Danger abounds, so duty abounds!

Some wonder if we are in danger of becoming too confessional. Others worry we are becoming too broad. Some worry we're too wrapped up in doctrine that we fail to share the good news. Others worry we don't worry about doctrine enough and so we're in danger of losing the gospel. These extremes can be mischaracterizations, but they are both worth considering.

But we must be both confessional *and* missional if we want to be consistent with our history. We live in a time when fanciful interpretations of the text abound. It seems incumbent upon us in this present hour to clearly delineate where we will stand firm in the faith and act like men with courage — doing it all in love. We do these things not just to be orthodox, but in order to share with the world what is most dear — Jesus and his gospel. The present hour calls us to this work!

So how can we avoid being weak? How can we avoid being mean? How can we avoid being arrogant? What will help us hold dear the doctrine we believe? How can we stand firm while being hot-hearted in our evangelism? How can we be humble and cheerful Christians?

Well, we need to remember that we are forgiven Corinthians.

Who were you before you met the Savior from Galilee? If you think back, you should be reminded from 1 Corinthians 6 that sinners will not inherit the kingdom of God. And then Paul says, "and such were some of us, but we have been washed, we have been sanctified, we have been justified in the name of the Lord Jesus Christ and by the Spirit of our God" (1 Corinthians 6:11). Believers, we have found a righteousness not our own in the Man who took our place upon the tree, suffering the fate of the ungodly, taking the place of the weak and arrogant. At Calvary, as the great Baptist preacher R. G. Lee points out in his famous sermon *Payday Someday*, "Christ Jesus became for sinners all that God must judge so that we by faith in Him might become all that God cannot." May we remember we can only be alert and stand firm without stumbling because Another stood alert and firm without stumbling. And he certainly played the Man at Golgotha and rose on the third day in vindication.

Baptists, we should never be soft or squishy. We should never be angry or arrogant either. Have you ever thought about how you came to believe what you believe? For when it comes to who we are, "we have nothing that we have not received." When it comes to the things we hold most dear, we are drinking deeply from wells that we did not dig! For those of us who have become beneficiaries of the cross and who share in the power of the resurrection, we dare not be haughty or angry or scared. May we hold our beliefs dear, and may we hold them in a way that reflects how we came to know them in the first place, by grace.

Indeed, Corinth Baptist may not be the most popular name for a church. The Pillar Network I help to lead isn't rebranding as the Corinth Baptist Network anytime soon.

But you know what? It may not be the worst thing. For if we remember we are forgiven Corinthians, then it will make us happy and convictional and confessional and courageous and compassionate and cheerful because we are changed men and women.

As it turns out, being Baptists with a Corinthian flare isn't so bad after all.

Printed in the USA
CPSIA information can be obtained
at www.ICGtesting.com
LVHW021806221124
797377LV00003B/214